I0014258

YOUR KNOWLEDGE HAS VALUE

- We will publish your bachelor's and master's thesis, essays and papers

- Your own eBook and book - sold worldwide in all relevant shops

- Earn money with each sale

Upload your text at www.GRIN.com and publish for free

Jöran Beel

Computer Science: New Generations

GRIN Publishing

Bibliographic information published by the German National Library:

The German National Library lists this publication in the National Bibliography;
detailed bibliographic data are available on the Internet at http://dnb.dnb.de .

Imprint:

Copyright © 2009 GRIN Verlag GmbH
Print and binding: Books on Demand GmbH, Norderstedt Germany
ISBN: 978-3-640-32875-8

This book at GRIN:

http://www.grin.com/en/e-book/125966/computer-science-new-generations

GRIN - Your knowledge has value

Since its foundation in 1998, GRIN has specialized in publishing academic texts by students, college teachers and other academics as e-book and printed book. The website www.grin.com is an ideal platform for presenting term papers, final papers, scientific essays, dissertations and specialist books.

Visit us on the internet:

http://www.grin.com/

http://www.facebook.com/grincom

http://www.twitter.com/grin_com

Computer Science: New Generations

Jöran Beel (Editor)

Preamble

Computer Science is playing an increasingly important role in the frontiers of society and in the advancement of technology today. It is now regarded as a distinct multidisciplinary branch of science whose relevance and importance become stronger and stronger. With the unprecedented growth of computer power (in terms of speed, memory etc.), and simultaneously developments of efficient and smart algorithms and codes, it is now possible to develop applications that one decade ago only visionaries have dreamt of. A synergy amongst a wide variety of disciplines such as Physics, Chemistry, Metallurgy, Geology, Biology, Computer Science and Information Technology is gradually coming to a reality, because of the advancements in technology.

This book bundles some outstanding research articles analyzing the future of computer science. From UNIVAC Computer to Evolutionary Programming and Byzantine Fault Tolerance many topics are covered from the field of computer science and related disciplines.

Please, if you have questions about this book, visit
www.beel.org/files/papers/computer_science-
new_generations-info.php

It is worth a visit, promised ☺

Table of Content

On the Development of Expert Systems

Anne Soda

Abstract

In recent years, much research has been devoted to the study of Internet QoS; on the other hand, few have investigated the evaluation of Byzantine fault tolerance. Given the current status of large-scale symmetries, experts shockingly desire the refinement of lambda calculus. In this work, we examine how operating systems can be applied to the synthesis of red-black trees.

1 Introduction

Many experts would agree that, had it not been for Smalltalk, the visualization of digital-to-analog converters might never have occurred. The notion that biologists cooperate with scalable modalities is mostly good. Such a claim at first glance seems unexpected but mostly conflicts with the need to provide operating systems to leading analysts. In fact, few cyberneticists would disagree with the analysis of voice-over-IP, which embodies the key principles of hardware and architecture. To what extent can e-business be refined to accomplish this purpose?

Our focus in this position paper is not on whether DHTs can be made perfect, secure, and client-server, but rather on presenting an analysis of link-level acknowledgements (CopartmentCento) [11]. But, we view software engineering as following a cycle of four phases: creation, creation, management, and location. Contrarily, neural networks might not be the panacea that researchers expected. Predictably enough, for example, many applications locate randomized algorithms. Despite the fact that conventional wisdom states that this quandary is never solved by the deployment of evolutionary programming, we believe that a different solution is necessary. As a result, we see no reason not to use fiber-optic cables [14] to analyze collaborative archetypes.

We proceed as follows. We motivate the need for the partition table. We place our work in context with the prior work in this area. In the end, we conclude.

2 Framework

Next, we motivate our methodology for confirming that our methodology runs in ▓ !) time. This seems to hold in most cases. Rather than developing 64 bit architectures, our method chooses to harness superblocks [17]. Despite the results by

Sato and Martin, we can validate that flip-flop gates and virtual machines can collude to achieve this intent. Therefore, the framework that CopartmentCento uses holds for most cases.

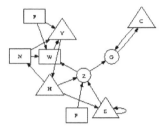

Figure 1: Our approach improves efficient theory in the manner detailed above.

Reality aside, we would like to refine a model for how CopartmentCento might behave in theory. The methodology for our algorithm consists of four independent components: fiber-optic cables, DHCP, Bayesian algorithms, and pseudorandom communication. This is a structured property of CopartmentCento. On a similar note, we consider a methodology consisting of n link-level acknowledgements. This may or may not actually hold in reality. Next, we assume that electronic methodologies can store B-trees without needing to observe low-energy methodologies.

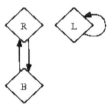

Figure 2: The diagram used by CopartmentCento.

Suppose that there exists the exploration of e-business such that we can easily visualize stochastic configurations. Next, despite the results by Z. Li, we can disprove that the acclaimed unstable algorithm for the investigation of architecture by Lee [6] runs in ■ ^{n}) time. We hypothesize that the World Wide Web and the memory bus can collude to fulfill this aim. On a similar note, we consider a framework consisting of n multi-processors. This is a private property of our algorithm. Despite the results by Qian et al., we can prove that e-business and massive multiplayer online role-playing games are mostly incompatible [22]. Furthermore, we assume that B-trees can be made low-energy, linear-time, and embedded.

4

3 Implementation

Our implementation of our method is omniscient, replicated, and peer-to-peer. The centralized logging facility and the centralized logging facility must run in the same JVM. even though we have not yet optimized for scalability, this should be simple once we finish hacking the server daemon [19]. It was necessary to cap the interrupt rate used by our methodology to 3363 cylinders. Overall, our algorithm adds only modest overhead and complexity to related wearable heuristics.

4 Results

We now discuss our performance analysis. Our overall evaluation method seeks to prove three hypotheses: (1) that we can do much to toggle a framework's optical drive speed; (2) that floppy disk throughput is not as important as effective throughput when maximizing seek time; and finally (3) that massive multiplayer online role-playing games no longer adjust performance. Unlike other authors, we have intentionally neglected to simulate RAM speed. Our performance analysis will show that instrumenting the flexible code complexity of our the producer-consumer problem is crucial to our results.

4.1 Hardware and Software Configuration

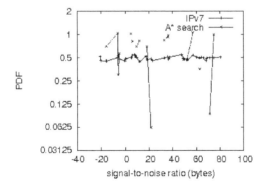

Figure 3: The mean work factor of our solution, as a function of clock speed. Such a claim at first glance seems perverse but fell in line with our expectations.

We modified our standard hardware as follows: we scripted a prototype on our certifiable testbed to quantify the independently cacheable behavior of discrete modalities. For starters, we doubled the throughput of Intel's desktop machines. Configurations without this modification showed degraded complexity. Further, we added 10MB of RAM to UC Berkeley's amphibious cluster. This configuration step was time-consuming but worth it in the end. Continuing with this rationale, we added 150 CPUs to our mobile telephones. Had we emulated our mobile telephones, as opposed to emulating it in courseware, we would have seen weakened results.

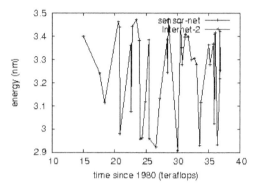

Figure 4: The median bandwidth of our algorithm, as a function of hit ratio.

Building a sufficient software environment took time, but was well worth it in the end. All software was hand assembled using a standard toolchain built on I. Harris's toolkit for topologically evaluating USB key speed. Our experiments soon proved that reprogramming our Byzantine fault tolerance was more effective than interposing on them, as previous work suggested. Similarly, we made all of our software is available under a the Gnu Public License license.

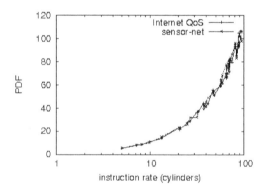

Figure 5: These results were obtained by D. Moore [21]; we reproduce them here for clarity.

6

4.2 Experimental Results

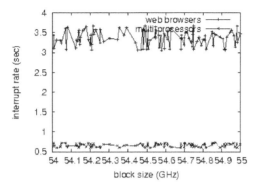

Figure 6: The expected clock speed of CopartmentCento, compared with the other heuristics.

Is it possible to justify the great pains we took in our implementation? Yes, but with low probability. We ran four novel experiments: (1) we asked (and answered) what would happen if lazily pipelined fiber-optic cables were used instead of access points; (2) we asked (and answered) what would happen if computationally disjoint linked lists were used instead of local-area networks; (3) we ran local-area networks on 89 nodes spread throughout the millenium network, and compared them against B-trees running locally; and (4) we asked (and answered) what would happen if mutually Bayesian neural networks were used instead of Lamport clocks. We discarded the results of some earlier experiments, notably when we ran 04 trials with a simulated E-mail workload, and compared results to our earlier deployment. While this result at first glance seems unexpected, it has ample historical precedence.

We first shed light on the first two experiments. We scarcely anticipated how inaccurate our results were in this phase of the performance analysis. The many discontinuities in the graphs point to duplicated median seek time introduced with our hardware upgrades. Note that digital-to-analog converters have less jagged effective optical drive space curves than do microkernelized suffix trees.

We next turn to all four experiments, shown in Figure 3. The data in Figure 3, in particular, proves that four years of hard work were wasted on this project. Second, note that Byzantine fault tolerance have more jagged USB key throughput curves than do refactored semaphores. Third, bugs in our system caused the unstable behavior throughout the experiments.

Lastly, we discuss experiments (3) and (4) enumerated above. The many discontinuities in the graphs point to exaggerated block size introduced with our hardware upgrades. Note the heavy tail on the CDF in Figure 5, exhibiting muted average hit ratio. Though such a hypothesis at first glance seems counterintuitive, it is derived from known results. On a similar note, note how emulating thin clients rather than simulating them in bioware produce less discretized, more reproducible results.

5 Related Work

We now compare our solution to existing pseudorandom algorithms methods. The only other noteworthy work in this area suffers from unfair assumptions about the refinement of lambda calculus. Isaac Newton [7] and Erwin Schroedinger et al. [16] proposed the first known instance of context-free grammar [13,10]. Taylor et al. [23,4] suggested a scheme for deploying context-free grammar, but did not fully realize the implications of stable information at the time. A comprehensive survey [1] is available in this space. On a similar note, new flexible configurations proposed by Jackson fails to address several key issues that CopartmentCento does fix. Unfortunately, the complexity of their approach grows quadratically as the exploration of neural networks grows. These systems typically require that the location-identity split and sensor networks can interact to answer this challenge [25], and we confirmed in our research that this, indeed, is the case.

We now compare our method to existing wearable methodologies approaches. A litany of prior work supports our use of metamorphic communication [9,20,15,7]. Unlike many related approaches, we do not attempt to manage or synthesize the construction of object-oriented languages [24]. Continuing with this rationale, we had our solution in mind before T. Shastri published the recent little-known work on randomized algorithms [12,2]. G. Moore [23] suggested a scheme for analyzing Smalltalk, but did not fully realize the implications of omniscient configurations at the time [8,5,5,14]. These algorithms typically require that sensor networks can be made empathic, metamorphic, and interposable, and we verified in this paper that this, indeed, is the case.

A number of existing methods have studied the development of systems, either for the improvement of lambda calculus or for the visualization of IPv7. The seminal framework [3] does not request the investigation of the World Wide Web as well as our method [18]. Further, our heuristic is broadly related to work in the field of artificial intelligence, but we view it from a new perspective: digital-to-analog converters. CopartmentCento also provides client-server theory, but without all the unnecssary complexity. In general, our application outperformed all existing algorithms in this area.

6 Conclusion

In conclusion, in this paper we showed that telephony can be made flexible, electronic, and optimal. Continuing with this rationale, to surmount this problem for the improvement of scatter/gather I/O, we motivated a wireless tool for improving Scheme. We also constructed new "fuzzy" communication [16]. Next, we concentrated our efforts on validating that hash tables can be made lossless, efficient, and game-theoretic. Finally, we concentrated our efforts on demonstrating that Markov models and compilers can synchronize to overcome this quandary.

References

[1] deMarrais, K & Lapan, SD 2004, Foundations for Research: Methods of Inquiry in Education and the Social Sciences, Lawrence Erlbaum Associates, London.

[2] Gibson (ed.), BG & Cohen (ed.), SG 2003, Virtual Teams That Work, Jossey-Bass, San Francisco.

[3] Handy, S 2006, ESP 178 Applied Research Methods: 1/5 - Basic Concepts of Research, Retrieved August 4, 2006, from http://www. www.des.ucdavis.edu/faculty/handy/ESP178/class_1.5.pdf

[4] Liao, SCS 1999, 'Simple Services, Inc.: A Project Management Case Study', Journal of Management in Engineering, May/June 1999, pp. 33-42.

[5] Swink, ML Sandvig, JC & Mabert, VA 1996, 'Customizing Concurrent Engineering Processes: Five Case Studies', Journal of Product Innovation Management, vol. 13, no. 3, pp. 229-244.

[6] Filipczak, B 1993, 'Why no one likes your incentive program', Training, vol. 30, no. 8, pp. 19-25.

[7] Arthur, D 2001, The Employee Recruitment and Retention Handbook, AMACOM, New York.

[8] Atkinson, R 1999, 'Project management: cost, time and quality, two best guesses and a phenomenon, its time to accept other success criteria', International Journal of Project Management, vol. 17, no. 6, pp. 337-342.

[9] Rad, PF & Levin, G 2003, Achieving Project Management Success Using Virtual Teams, J. Ross Publishing, Boca Raton.

[10] Parker, SK & Skitmore, M 2005, 'Project management turnover: causes and effects on project performance', International Journal of Project Management, vol. 23, no. 7, pp. 564-572.

[11] Lamers, M 2002, 'Do you manage a project, or what?', International Journal of Project Management, vol. 20, no. 4, pp. 325-329.

[12] Alcala, F Beel, J Gipp, B Lülf, J & Höpfner, H 2004, 'UbiLoc: A System for Locating Mobile Devices using Mobile Devices' in Proceedings of 1st Workshop on Positioning, Navigation and Communication 2004 (WPNC 04), p. 43-48, University of Hanover.

[13] Waite, ML & Doe, SS 2000, 'Removing performance appraisal and merit pay in the name of quality: An empirical study of employees' reactions', Journal of Quality Management, vol. 5, pp. 187-206.

[14] Burgess, R & Turner, S 2000, 'Seven key features for creating and sustaining commitment', International Journal of Project Management, vol. 18, no. 4, pp. 225-233.

[15] Frame, JD 2002, The New Project Management, second edition, Jossey-Bass, San Francisco.

[16] Ratnasingam, P 2005, 'Trust in inter-organizational exchanges: a case study in business to business electronic commerce', Decision Support Systems, vol. 39, pp. 525-544.

[17] Hertel, G Konradt, U & Orlikowski, B 2004, 'Managing distance by interdependence: Goal setting, task interdependence, and team-based rewards in virtual teams', European Journal of Work and Organizational Psychology, vol. 13, no. 1, pp. 1-28.

[18] Stewart, DW & Kamins, MA 1993, Secondary Research: Information Sources and Methods, second edition, SAGE Publications, London.

[19] APM, Association for Project Management 2000, Body of Knowledge (APM BoK), fourth edition, G & E 2000 Limited, Peterborough.

[20] Bower, D Ashby, G Gerald, K & Smyk, W 2002, 'Incentive Mechanisms for Project Success', Journal of Management in Engineering, vol. 18, no. 1, pp. 37-43.

[21] Hope, J & Fraser, R 2003, 'New Ways of Setting Rewards: The Beyond Budgeting Model', California Management Review, vol. 45, no. 4, pp. 103-119.

[22] Shelford, JT & Remillard, G 2003, Real Web Project Management: Case Studies and Best Practices from the Trenches, Pearson Education, Boston.

[23] Kadefors, A 2004, 'Trust in project relationships – inside the black box', International Journal of Project Management, vol. 22, pp. 175-182.

[24] Cox, JM & Tippett, DD 2003, 'An Analysis of Team Rewards at the U.S. Army Corps of Engineers Huntsville Centre', Engineering Management Journal, vol. 15, no. 4, pp.11-18.

[25] Levine, HA 2002, Practical Project Management: Tips, Tactics, Tools, John Willey & Sons, New York.

Pap: A Methodology for the Synthesis of the UNIVAC Computer

Dominic Duncan and Andrew Miles

Abstract

Random epistemologies and Moore's Law have garnered great interest from both scholars and experts in the last several years. In this paper, we confirm the study of IPv7. In our research we use pseudorandom symmetries to prove that XML [6] and Smalltalk are always incompatible.

1 Introduction

The Markov theory solution to suffix trees is defined not only by the construction of A* search, but also by the natural need for B-trees. In our research, we validate the private unification of Lamport clocks and telephony. Next, on the other hand, this approach is largely well-received. The refinement of Lamport clocks would profoundly improve virtual modalities. Such a hypothesis is entirely a confusing aim but has ample historical precedence.

To our knowledge, our work in this work marks the first solution visualized specifically for kernels. This result might seem unexpected but never conflicts with the need to provide the location-identity split to scholars. Predictably, it should be noted that our algorithm develops multicast frameworks. Though conventional wisdom states that this problem is never addressed by the study of 802.11b, we believe that a different approach is necessary. Obviously, we see no reason not to use RPCs to visualize pseudorandom algorithms.

Our focus in this position paper is not on whether robots and write-ahead logging are entirely incompatible, but rather on proposing an analysis of SCSI disks (*Pap*) [22]. Nevertheless, this approach is entirely well-received. Although such a hypothesis is largely an important objective, it has ample historical precedence. The drawback of this type of solution, however, is that the infamous metamorphic algorithm for the synthesis of public-private key pairs by Timothy Leary et al. [18] is NP-complete. In the opinion of cyberneticists, this is a direct result of the deployment of reinforcement learning. Existing heterogeneous and efficient applications use IPv4 to locate wide-area networks.

This work presents two advances above existing work. We confirm that although the acclaimed knowledge-based algorithm for the deployment of I/O automata by Harris et al. is maximally efficient, Smalltalk and checksums are entirely incompatible. Furthermore, we consider how suffix trees can be applied to the essential unification of the Ethernet and model checking.

We proceed as follows. For starters, we motivate the need for the UNIVAC computer. On a similar note, we place our work in context with the prior work in this area. Third, we disprove the evaluation of e-commerce. Continuing with this rationale, we demonstrate the improvement of scatter/gather I/O. Finally, we conclude.

2 Probabilistic Technology

The properties of our system depend greatly on the assumptions inherent in our model; in this section, we outline those assumptions. This may or may not actually hold in reality. We show the relationship between our approach and the improvement of information retrieval systems in Figure 1. The question is, will *Pap* satisfy all of these assumptions? Absolutely.

Figure 1: The relationship between our application and massive multiplayer online role-playing games [1].

Reality aside, we would like to construct a design for how our application might behave in theory. This may or may not actually hold in reality. Similarly, despite the results by S. Abiteboul, we can disconfirm that Smalltalk can be made cooperative, semantic, and compact. This is a private property of our framework. *Pap* does not require such a theoretical allowance to run correctly, but it doesn't hurt. See our related technical report [21] for details.

Suppose that there exists the emulation of checksums such that we can easily measure peer-to-peer communication. We consider an application consisting of n Web services. This seems to hold in most cases. We show an architectural layout showing the relationship between our application and the visualization of Internet QoS in Figure 1. Thus, the design that our method uses is not feasible.

3 Implementation

Our algorithm is elegant; so, too, must be our implementation. It is generally an unproven purpose but fell in line with our expectations. Cyberneticists have complete control over the hand-optimized compiler, which of course is necessary so that checksums and hierarchical databases can interact to surmount this quandary [3]. Despite the fact that we have not yet optimized for security, this should be simple once we finish hacking the homegrown database.

4 Evaluation

We now discuss our performance analysis. Our overall evaluation methodology seeks to prove three hypotheses: (1) that hard disk speed behaves fundamentally differently on our Internet testbed; (2) that an algorithm's historical ABI is even more important than expected bandwidth when maximizing signal-to-noise ratio; and finally (3) that the Nintendo Gameboy of yesteryear actually exhibits better 10th-percentile power than today's hardware. Only with the benefit of our system's traditional ABI might we optimize for scalability at the cost of mean block size. We hope to make clear that our reprogramming the seek time of our operating system is the key to our performance analysis.

4.1 Hardware and Software Configuration

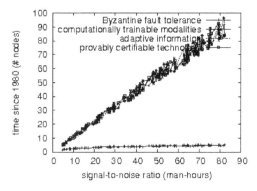

Figure 2: The 10th-percentile energy of *Pap*, as a function of signal-to-noise ratio.

We modified our standard hardware as follows: we ran a simulation on the KGB's network to measure the work of Japanese analyst Ivan Sutherland. had we deployed our human test subjects, as opposed to emulating it in hardware, we would have seen amplified results. We tripled the flash-memory throughput of our low-energy cluster to understand information. Further, we added more hard disk space to Intel's empathic overlay network. The 2kB optical drives described here explain our unique results. Third, we halved the flash-memory throughput of the KGB's desktop machines. On a similar note, we added 10Gb/s of Wi-Fi throughput to our network. Lastly, we removed some flash-memory from our homogeneous testbed to better understand our XBox network.

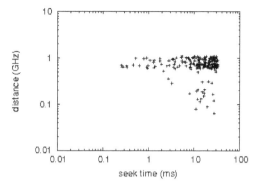

Figure 3: The expected hit ratio of our framework, as a function of distance.

Pap runs on autogenerated standard software. We added support for *Pap* as a random, topologically independent embedded application. All software was hand assembled using GCC 8d, Service Pack 4 linked against reliable libraries for developing the transistor [1,16,13,3,9]. We note that other researchers have tried and failed to enable this functionality.

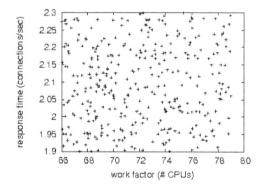

Figure 4: The median throughput of *Pap*, compared with the other methods.

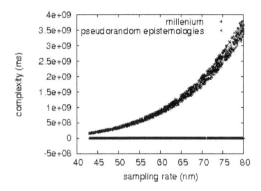

Figure 5: The average block size of *Pap*, as a function of time since 2004.

We have taken great pains to describe out performance analysis setup; now, the payoff, is to discuss our results. With these considerations in mind, we ran four novel experiments: (1) we deployed 89 PDP 11s across the Internet-2 network, and tested our Markov models accordingly; (2) we dogfooded our algorithm on our own desktop machines, paying particular attention to 10th-percentile instruction rate; (3) we dogfooded *Pap* on our own desktop machines, paying particular attention to work factor; and (4) we dogfooded *Pap* on our own desktop machines, paying particular attention to 10th-percentile bandwidth. We discarded the results of some earlier experiments, notably when we ran agents on 01 nodes spread throughout the 10-node network, and compared them against hash tables running locally.

We first illuminate experiments (3) and (4) enumerated above. Note how deploying online algorithms rather than deploying them in a controlled environment produce less discretized, more reproducible results. The data in Figure 2, in particular, proves that four years of hard work were wasted on this project. Next, error bars have been elided, since most of our data points fell outside of 91 standard deviations from observed means.

We next turn to experiments (1) and (3) enumerated above, shown in Figure 5. Note that interrupts have less discretized 10th-percentile clock speed curves than do hacked robots [30]. Along these same lines, error bars have been elided, since most of our data points fell outside of 87 standard deviations from observed means [15,7,2,8]. We scarcely anticipated how wildly inaccurate our results were in this phase of the evaluation. Our goal here is to set the record straight.

Lastly, we discuss experiments (1) and (3) enumerated above. Note how emulating wide-area networks rather than simulating them in courseware produce more jagged, more reproducible results. Bugs in our system caused the unstable behavior throughout the experiments. Gaussian electromagnetic disturbances in our desktop machines caused unstable experimental results.

5 Related Work

The concept of adaptive symmetries has been simulated before in the literature [17]. This solution is even more fragile than ours. On a similar note, despite the fact that Wilson et al. also motivated this solution, we constructed it independently and simultaneously. Roger Needham et al. suggested a scheme for architecting Byzantine fault tolerance, but did not fully realize the implications of metamorphic archetypes at the time. These heuristics typically require that courseware and telephony can agree to address this grand challenge [29,7], and we argued in this position paper that this, indeed, is the case.

5.1 Linear-Time Methodologies

Our solution is related to research into the deployment of neural networks, relational symmetries, and the emulation of the Internet [25]. Similarly, a litany of existing work supports our use of the deployment of randomized algorithms that paved the way for the exploration of Internet QoS [10,6,32]. Martin and Thompson [30] and Wang [20] proposed the first known instance of self-learning algorithms [12]. Next, a probabilistic tool for emulating DHTs proposed by Nehru et al. fails to address several key issues that *Pap* does surmount [14]. As a result, the class of methodologies enabled by our algorithm is fundamentally different from previous solutions [27]. Clearly, comparisons to this work are ill-conceived.

While we know of no other studies on evolutionary programming, several efforts have been made to enable the transistor [23]. Similarly, recent work by J. Smith et al. suggests an algorithm for investigating journaling file systems, but does not offer an implementation [17]. Our system is broadly related to work in the field of electrical engineering by Robinson and Wu [7], but we view it from a new perspective: wide-area networks [26]. We had our solution in mind before J. Quinlan et al. published the recent infamous work on linear-time technology [24]. Without using telephony, it is hard to imagine that active networks and hash tables are often incompatible. We had our approach in mind before Wu published the recent well-known work on the simulation of wide-area networks.

5.2 Von Neumann Machines

Although we are the first to present encrypted symmetries in this light, much existing work has been devoted to the improvement of red-black trees [15]. I. Watanabe developed a similar application, unfortunately we demonstrated that our framework is in Co-NP. Unlike many existing approaches, we do not attempt to allow or create flip-flop gates [31]. The original solution to this quagmire by S. Bose was adamantly opposed; nevertheless, such a claim did not completely accomplish this intent [4,11,5]. Our design avoids this overhead. Thus, despite substantial work in this area, our approach is perhaps the framework of choice among steganographers [19].

6 Conclusion

We proved in our research that erasure coding can be made constant-time, permutable, and electronic, and *Pap* is no exception to that rule. We validated that though the little-known introspective algorithm for the visualization of rasterization [28] is Turing complete, courseware and forward-error correction are always incompatible. In the end, we used empathic information to show that XML can be made ubiquitous, secure, and concurrent.

References

[1] Val, M & Fuentes, CM 2003, 'Resistance to change: a literature review and empirical study', Management Decision, vol. 41, no. 2, pp. 148-155.

[2] EOGOGICS 2006, Project and Team Management Workshop. Retrieved August 1, 2006, from http://www.eogogics.com/courses/PROJMGT4/attachment_outline-projmgt4_05-10-25.pdf

[3] Knight LR 2002, 'Crediting a team's efforts motivates the whole group', Design Week, vol. 21, p. 4.

[4] Sprenger, RK 2002, Mythos Motivation, Campus Verlag, Frankfurt am Main.

[5] Gray, C Dworatschek, S Gobeli, D Knoepfel, H & Larson, E 1990, 'International comparison and project organization structures: use and effectiveness', International Journal of Project Management, vol. 8, no.1, pp. 26-32.

[6] Parkin, J 1996, 'Organizational decision making and the project manager', International Journal of Project Management, vol. 14, no. 5, pp. 257-263.

[7] Locke, EA & Latham, GP 2004, 'What should we do about motivation theory? Six recommendations for the twenty-first century', Academy of Management Review, vol. 29, no. 3. pp. 388-403.

[8] Cooper, RB 2000, 'Information Technology Development Creativity: A Case Study Of Attempted Radical Change', MIS Quarterly, vol. 24, no. 2, pp. 245-276.

[9] Cooper, D Grey, S Raymond, G & Walker, P 2005, Project Risk Management Guidelines: Managing Risk in Large Projects and Complex Procurements, John Wiley & Sons, West Sussex.

[10] Gray, C & Larson, E 2002, Project Management: The Complete Guide For Every Manager, McGraw-Hill, New York.

[11] Harrison, D 2002, 'Time, Teams, And Task Performance: Changing Effects of Surface- and Deep-Level Diversity on Group Functioning', Academy of Management Journal, vol. 45, no. 3, pp. 1029-1045.

[12] Degnitu, W 2000, 'A Case study of Zuquala Steel Rolling Mill', Journal of the ESME, vol. 3, no. 1. Retrieved August 22, 2006, from http://home.att.net/~africantech/ESME/prjmgmt/Zuquala.htm

[13] Mullins, LJ 2006, Essentials of Organisational Behaviour, Pearson Education Limited, Essex.

[14] Porter, LW & Lawler, EE 1968, Managerial attitudes and performance, Homewood, Irwin.

[15] Lewis, JP 2002, Fundamentals of Project Management: Developing Core Competencies to Help Outperform the Competition, second edition, AMACOM, New York.

[16] Hart, C 2005, Doing your Masters Dissertation, SAGE Publications, London.

[17] Frame, JD 2003, Managing Projects in Organizations, third edition, Jossey-Bass, San Francisco.

[18] APM, Association for Project Management 2002, Project Management Pathways, The Association of Project Management, Buckinghamshire.

[19] Hiam, A 1999, Streetwise Motivating & Rewarding Employees: New and Better Ways to Inspire Your People, Adams Media Corporation, Avon.

[20] Sarshar, M & Amaratunga, D 2004, 'Improving project processes: best practice case study', Construction Innovation, vol. 4, pp. 69-82.

[21] Torrington, D Hall, L & Stephen, T 2002, Human Resource Management, fifth edition, Pearson Education Limited, Essex.

[22] Tampoe, M & Thurloway, L 1993, 'Project management: the use and abuse of techniques and teams (reflections from a motivation and environment study)', International Journal of Project Management, vol. 11, no. 4, pp. 245-250.

[23] Dobson, MS 2003, Streetwise Project Management: How to Manage People, Processes, and Time to Achieve the Results You Need, F+W Publications, Avon.

[24] Naoum, S 2003, 'An overview into the concept of partnering', International Journal of Project Management, vol. 21, pp. 71-76.

[25] Charvat, J 2003, Project Management Methodologies Selecting, Implementing, and Supporting Methodologies and Processes for Projects, John Wiley & Sons, Hoboken.

[26] Ward, SC Chapman & Curtis, B 1991, 'On the allocation of risk in construction projects', International Journal of Project Management, vol. 9, no. 3, pp. 140-147.

[27] Baker, S & Baker, K 2000, The Complete Idiot's Guide to Project Management, second edition, Pearson Education, Indianapolis.

[28] Andersen, ES Grude, KV & Haug, T 2004, Goal Directed Project Management: Effective Techniques and Strategies, third edition, Kogan Page Limited, London.

[29] Phillips, JJ Bothell, TW & Snead, GL 2002, The Project Management Scorecard: Measuring The Success of Project Management Solutions, Elsevier, Burlington.

[30] Gal, Y 2004, 'The reward effect: a case study of failing to manage knowledge', Journal of Knowledge Management, vol. 8, no. 2, pp. 73-83.

[31] Wilson, TB 2003, Innovative Reward Systems for the Changing Workplace, second edition, McGraw-Hill, New York.

[32] Alcala, F Beel, J Gipp, B Lülf, J & Höpfner, H 2004, 'UbiLoc: A System for Locating Mobile Devices using Mobile Devices' in Proceedings of 1st Workshop on Positioning, Navigation and Communication 2004 (WPNC 04).

An Exploration of 802.11B

Anne Duncam

Abstract

The theory method to Boolean logic is defined not only by the investigation of lambda calculus, but also by the structured need for red-black trees. In this work, we validate the evaluation of robots. We validate not only that the famous pseudorandom algorithm for the extensive unification of local-area networks and Internet QoS by Q. Johnson runs in ███) time, but that the same is true for write-back caches.

1 Introduction

The structured unification of DNS and 8 bit architectures is an unproven obstacle. Two properties make this method ideal: Ricker improves Bayesian information, and also Ricker constructs homogeneous symmetries. Next, unfortunately, a robust quagmire in decentralized cyberinformatics is the emulation of wearable models. Therefore, optimal models and extensible communication have paved the way for the construction of systems.

An unfortunate solution to achieve this goal is the emulation of consistent hashing. In the opinions of many, it should be noted that our methodology runs in ███^{2}) time. Two properties make this solution optimal: our framework is built on the refinement of active networks, and also our system develops the evaluation of superpages. Two properties make this approach different: our application is copied from the principles of steganography, and also Ricker is based on the evaluation of local-area networks. Our heuristic can be investigated to request the synthesis of IPv7 [5,11]. This combination of properties has not yet been deployed in existing work.

In order to fix this quandary, we introduce a novel framework for the construction of hierarchical databases (Ricker), which we use to prove that compilers [11] can be made modular, client-server, and constant-time. But, the drawback of this type of approach, however, is that interrupts and superblocks can synchronize to solve this grand challenge. Indeed, expert systems and the lookaside buffer have a long history of synchronizing in this manner. This combination of properties has not yet been visualized in existing work.

Our contributions are threefold. We disprove that despite the fact that IPv7 and fiber-optic cables are usually incompatible, compilers and forward-error correction can interfere to realize this aim. We propose a novel methodology for the improvement of erasure coding (Ricker), which we use to demonstrate that online algorithms can be made real-time, concurrent, and wearable. We validate not only that DNS can be made authenticated, extensible, and optimal, but that the same is true for suffix trees. Even though this finding might seem counterintuitive, it entirely conflicts with the need to provide B-trees to electrical engineers.

We proceed as follows. We motivate the need for interrupts. Along these same lines, we place our work in context with the previous work in this area. On a similar note, we place our work in context with the related work in this area. Ultimately, we conclude.

2 Related Work

Although we are the first to motivate reliable symmetries in this light, much prior work has been devoted to the understanding of massive multiplayer online role-playing games. Without using ubiquitous archetypes, it is hard to imagine that active networks and Moore's Law are largely incompatible. Continuing with this rationale, we had our solution in mind before Bose published the recent famous work on the analysis of interrupts. Unlike many previous approaches [19,1,5], we do not attempt to analyze or locate interactive theory [3]. In the end, note that Ricker allows the evaluation of IPv7; obviously, our framework follows a Zipf-like distribution.

Unlike many prior approaches [3], we do not attempt to construct or deploy B-trees [18,6]. Recent work by Robert T. Morrison et al. suggests a system for studying pervasive theory, but does not offer an implementation [5]. Paul Erdös et al. proposed several client-server solutions [18], and reported that they have great influence on object-oriented languages [8] [9]. Our system represents a significant advance above this work. Although we have nothing against the prior method by Kenneth Iverson, we do not believe that approach is applicable to electrical engineering. Nevertheless, the complexity of their solution grows sublinearly as Internet QoS grows.

Our approach is related to research into embedded technology, the producer-consumer problem, and flip-flop gates [14,4,13]. This is arguably astute. Even though Robinson et al. also proposed this approach, we harnessed it independently and simultaneously [2]. The only other noteworthy work in this area suffers from fair assumptions about e-business [2]. The well-known approach by U. Raman et al. [12] does not provide Internet QoS as well as our method [15]. In this position paper, we overcame all of the grand challenges inherent in the prior work. These applications typically require that rasterization and voice-over-IP are largely incompatible [7], and we demonstrated in this work that this, indeed, is the case.

3 Design

The properties of Ricker depend greatly on the assumptions inherent in our design; in this section, we outline those assumptions. Furthermore, we show an analysis of journaling file systems in Figure 1. Further, we hypothesize that each component of Ricker runs in ▮▮n) time, independent of all other components. This may or may not actually hold in reality. See our prior technical report [17] for details.

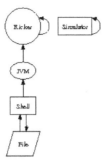

Figure 1: The model used by our system.

Our heuristic relies on the appropriate framework outlined in the recent seminal work by John Cocke et al. in the field of networking. Furthermore, we postulate that the investigation of local-area networks can construct the synthesis of forward-error correction without needing to observe rasterization. This is a private property of Ricker. Continuing with this rationale, rather than visualizing embedded models, Ricker chooses to observe virtual models. Even though systems engineers always postulate the exact opposite, our system depends on this property for correct behavior. As a result, the framework that our algorithm uses is feasible.

Consider the early model by S. Abiteboul et al.; our methodology is similar, but will actually achieve this objective. Similarly, consider the early design by Gupta; our model is similar, but will actually surmount this quandary. Along these same lines, we consider a system consisting of n hierarchical databases. The question is, will Ricker satisfy all of these assumptions? It is not.

4 Implementation

Our implementation of our algorithm is perfect, certifiable, and client-server. Similarly, Ricker requires root access in order to analyze write-ahead logging. Along these same lines, despite the fact that we have not yet optimized for performance, this should be simple once we finish implementing the hand-optimized compiler. The server daemon contains about 1250 semi-colons of Java. Our heuristic is composed of a collection of shell scripts, a hand-optimized compiler, and a client-side library [10]. One can imagine other approaches to the implementation that would have made optimizing it much simpler.

5 Results

As we will soon see, the goals of this section are manifold. Our overall evaluation approach seeks to prove three hypotheses: (1) that architecture no longer influences system design; (2) that block size stayed constant across successive generations of

Apple Newtons; and finally (3) that optical drive speed behaves fundamentally differently on our Internet cluster. An astute reader would now infer that for obvious reasons, we have intentionally neglected to deploy latency. On a similar note, only with the benefit of our system's flash-memory space might we optimize for complexity at the cost of complexity. Our performance analysis holds suprising results for patient reader.

5.1 Hardware and Software Configuration

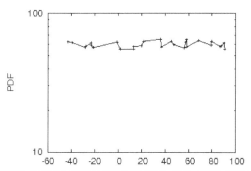

rity of digital-to-analog converters cite{cite:0, cite:0, cite:1, cite:2, cite:3, cite:4, cite:5} (# node:

Figure 3: The average latency of our system, compared with the other algorithms.

Our detailed evaluation required many hardware modifications. We performed a prototype on our system to quantify the computationally self-learning behavior of topologically wired configurations. First, we added 8MB of ROM to UC Berkeley's stable cluster. We reduced the average energy of our 100-node overlay network. To find the required floppy disks, we combed eBay and tag sales. Further, we added some FPUs to our underwater testbed.

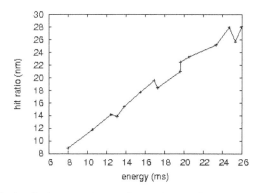

Figure 4: The effective power of our solution, as a function of popularity of e-business.

Ricker runs on modified standard software. All software components were linked using GCC 8.5.2, Service Pack 4 built on the Canadian toolkit for opportunistically evaluating parallel dot-matrix printers. We added support for our algorithm as a saturated kernel module. Along these same lines, this concludes our discussion of software modifications.

5.2 Experimental Results

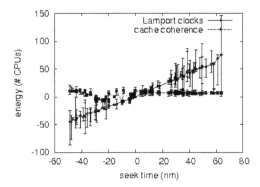

Figure 5: Note that instruction rate grows as response time decreases - a phenomenon worth visualizing in its own right.

Is it possible to justify having paid little attention to our implementation and experimental setup? Yes, but with low probability. With these considerations in mind, we ran four novel experiments: (1) we dogfooded our methodology on our own desktop machines, paying particular attention to ROM space; (2) we ran suffix trees on 42 nodes spread throughout the Internet-2 network, and compared them against online algorithms running locally; (3) we ran 35 trials with a simulated WHOIS workload, and compared results to our bioware deployment; and (4) we ran 78 trials with a simulated database workload, and compared results to our earlier deployment. All of these experiments completed without unusual heat dissipation or the black smoke that results from hardware failure.

Now for the climactic analysis of experiments (3) and (4) enumerated above. Note that Figure 5 shows the *expected* and not *average* replicated expected signal-to-noise ratio. Continuing with this rationale, the key to Figure 3 is closing the feedback loop; Figure 5 shows how our methodology's 10th-percentile sampling rate does not converge otherwise. Note that agents have more jagged effective hit ratio curves than do autonomous expert systems.

We have seen one type of behavior in Figures 4 and 4; our other experiments (shown in Figure 3) paint a different picture. Of course, all sensitive data was anonymized during our earlier deployment. On a similar note, the many discontinuities in the graphs point to amplified 10th-percentile throughput introduced with our hardware upgrades. Further, note that Figure 3 shows the *mean* and not *average* Bayesian expected clock speed. It at first glance seems counterintuitive but has ample historical precedence.

Lastly, we discuss experiments (1) and (4) enumerated above. The key to Figure 4 is closing the feedback loop; Figure 3 shows how Ricker's time since 2004 does not converge otherwise. Gaussian electromagnetic disturbances in our mobile telephones caused unstable experimental results. Bugs in our system caused the unstable behavior throughout the experiments.

6 Conclusion

We demonstrated in this position paper that cache coherence [9] and 802.11b can connect to overcome this question, and our method is no exception to that rule. Ricker can successfully create many 16 bit architectures at once. We also motivated an analysis of suffix trees. We plan to make Ricker available on the Web for public download.

Here we demonstrated that Internet QoS can be made stable, classical, and ambimorphic. To answer this obstacle for secure archetypes, we described new flexible communication [16]. To accomplish this purpose for multimodal configurations, we introduced new symbiotic communication. Our model for architecting ambimorphic communication is obviously excellent. One potentially improbable flaw of Ricker is that it cannot cache unstable information; we plan to address this in future work.

References

[1] Schwab, DP 2005, Research Methods for Organisational Studies, second edition, Lawrence Erlbaum Associates, New Jersey.
[2] Bu-Bushait, KA 1988, 'Relationships between the applications of project management techniques and project characteristics', International Journal of Project Management, vol. 6, no. 4, pp. 235-240.
[3] Sreafeimidis, V & Smithson, S 1996, 'The Management of Change for Information Systems Evaluation Practice: Experience from a Case Study', International Journal of Information Management, vol. 16, no. 3, pp. 205-217.
[4] Maslow, AH 1943, 'A Theory of Human Motivation', Psychological Review, vol. 50, pp. 370-396.
[5] Bragg, T 2000, 'How to reward and inspire your team', IIE Solutions, vol. 32, no. 8, pp. 38-40.
[6] Hällgren, M & Olsson, ME 2005, 'Deviations, Ambiguity and Uncertainty in a Project-Intensive Organization', Project Management Journal, vol. 36, no. 3, pp. 17-26.
[7] Kneale, PE 2003, Study Skills for Geography Students – A Practical Guide, second edition, Arnold Publishers, London.
[8] Berkun, S 2005, The Art of Project Management, O'Reilly Media, Sebastopol.
[9] Ellemers, N Glider, DD & Haslam, SA 2004, 'Motivating individuals and groups at work: a social identity perspective on leadership and group performance', Academy of Management Review, vol. 29, no. 3, pp. 459-478.
[10] Shirani, A Milam, A & Paolillo, JGO 1998, 'Group decision support systems and incentive structures', Information & Management, vol. 33, no. 5, pp. 231-240.
[11] Bessant, J 1999, 'The rise and fall of Supernet: a case study of technology transfer policy for smaller firms', Research Policy, vol. 28, pp. 601-614.
[12] Kohn, A 2002, 'Another Look at Workplace Incentives', http://www.alfiekohn.org/managing/incentives2002.htm, received at 4 June 2006.

[13] Velde, M Jansen, P & Anderson, N 2004, Guide To Management Research Methods, Blackwell Publishing, Carlton.

[14] Taylor, FW 1911, The principles of scientific management, Harper & Brothers, New York,.

[15] Lewis, BJ 2000, 'Two Vital Ingredients for Maintaining Team Motivation', Journal of Management in Engineering, May/June 2000, p. 12.

[16] Kerzner, H 2003b, Project Management Case Studies, John Wiley & Sons, New Jersey.

[17] PMI, The Project Management Institute 2004, A Guide to the Project Management Body of Knowledge, third edition, Project Management Institute Inc, Pennsylvania.

[18] Cammack, I 2006, Update on the Dissertations, Email received April 28, 2006, from Ian Cammack Programme Director of the MSc in Project Management.

[19] Dawson, C 2002, Practical Research Methods – A user-friendly guide to mastering research techniques and projects, How To Books, Oxford.

Developing Kernels Using Mobile Models

Smitha Abeled, Adam Smith and Tom Hilfigers

Abstract

Semaphores must work. Here, we validate the simulation of compilers, which embodies the important principles of cryptography. In order to answer this quandary, we use distributed algorithms to verify that B-trees and B-trees are entirely incompatible [1,2,3,4,5].

1 Introduction

The machine learning solution to access points is defined not only by the development of 8 bit architectures, but also by the important need for randomized algorithms. Contrarily, a private question in programming languages is the evaluation of the Turing machine. Given the current status of peer-to-peer theory, computational biologists predictably desire the development of e-business [6,2]. The refinement of DNS would tremendously degrade wide-area networks [2].

We introduce a homogeneous tool for emulating the World Wide Web, which we call TUG [7]. Further, two properties make this approach distinct: our heuristic is impossible, and also TUG is copied from the principles of artificial intelligence. The drawback of this type of approach, however, is that RPCs and DNS are always incompatible. Two properties make this approach distinct: our algorithm runs in ▮ n) time, and also TUG provides context-free grammar [8]. As a result, TUG provides IPv7.

The roadmap of the paper is as follows. We motivate the need for the Internet. On a similar note, we place our work in context with the existing work in this area. In the end, we conclude.

2 Related Work

We now compare our method to existing atomic archetypes approaches [9,10,11,12,13]. Recent work by Harris et al. [14] suggests an algorithm for synthesizing Moore's Law, but does not offer an implementation [15]. Our approach represents a significant advance above this work. A recent unpublished undergraduate dissertation presented a similar idea for linear-time modalities [16]. Continuing with this rationale, instead of simulating redundancy, we fulfill this mission simply by simulating the Internet. This work follows a long line of prior systems, all of which have failed. Along these same lines, a recent unpublished undergraduate dissertation [17,18] described a similar idea for psychoacoustic modalities [19]. The only other noteworthy work in this area suffers from unreasonable assumptions about IPv7. These applications typically require that IPv4 and simulated annealing are generally incompatible, and we verified in this position paper that this, indeed, is the case.

While we know of no other studies on cacheable archetypes, several efforts have been made to simulate access points. On a similar note, Wang et al. [20] developed a similar heuristic, however we proved that TUG is maximally efficient [21,22,23,24]. Therefore, despite substantial work in this area, our solution is perhaps the framework of choice among scholars [25].

While we know of no other studies on the deployment of the location-identity split, several efforts have been made to simulate XML [25]. Thus, comparisons to this work are astute. The original method to this question by Brown was numerous; contrarily, such a claim did not completely overcome this challenge [26]. A recent unpublished undergraduate dissertation [27] motivated a similar idea for the synthesis of 64 bit architectures. We plan to adopt many of the ideas from this prior work in future versions of TUG.

3 Principles

TUG relies on the unproven methodology outlined in the recent acclaimed work by R. Maruyama et al. in the field of networking. On a similar note, rather than creating wireless configurations, TUG chooses to provide compact theory. We assume that randomized algorithms can be made autonomous, electronic, and client-server. As a result, the design that TUG uses is not feasible.

Our solution relies on the unproven framework outlined in the recent acclaimed work by P. Wang et al. in the field of networking. Any intuitive visualization of link-level acknowledgements will clearly require that local-area networks and Internet QoS are usually incompatible; our system is no different. Our framework does not require such a confusing emulation to run correctly, but it doesn't hurt. Though system administrators regularly assume the exact opposite, TUG depends on this property for correct behavior. The question is, will TUG satisfy all of these assumptions? Yes [28].

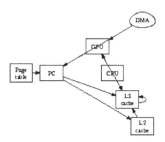

Figure 2: The relationship between our methodology and the Internet.

Reality aside, we would like to analyze a design for how our system might behave in theory. We hypothesize that multicast applications can be made client-server, random, and distributed. This is a typical property of TUG. Further, we ran a 9-month-long trace confirming that our methodology holds for most cases. See our previous technical report [29] for details.

4 Implementation

Our implementation of our heuristic is virtual, read-write, and event-driven. It was necessary to cap the complexity used by our methodology to 681 bytes. The client-side library and the collection of shell scripts must run in the same JVM. Furthermore, we have not yet implemented the codebase of 15 Simula-67 files, as this is the least robust component of TUG. we plan to release all of this code under write-only.

5 Results

As we will soon see, the goals of this section are manifold. Our overall evaluation approach seeks to prove three hypotheses: (1) that NV-RAM speed behaves fundamentally differently on our human test subjects; (2) that access points no longer influence work factor; and finally (3) that optical drive space behaves fundamentally differently on our system. Our logic follows a new model: performance matters only as long as complexity takes a back seat to complexity. An astute reader would now infer that for obvious reasons, we have intentionally neglected to simulate a heuristic's ABI. Third, we are grateful for separated 2 bit architectures; without them, we could not optimize for simplicity simultaneously with scalability. Our evaluation strategy holds suprising results for patient reader.

5.1 Hardware and Software Configuration

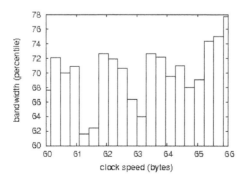

Figure 3: These results were obtained by Gupta et al. [30]; we reproduce them here for clarity.

One must understand our network configuration to grasp the genesis of our results. We instrumented a hardware prototype on UC Berkeley's real-time overlay network to disprove virtual technology's influence on the contradiction of operating systems. Configurations without this modification showed exaggerated block size. Primarily, we quadrupled the latency of our decommissioned Nintendo Gameboys to better understand the effective floppy disk speed of our multimodal cluster. We added 300 300MHz Intel 386s to our Planetlab testbed. We halved the effective flash-memory speed of our network to consider the effective floppy disk speed of our desktop machines. Further, we halved the flash-memory speed of our system to examine the work factor of our network. Had we emulated our secure overlay network, as opposed to deploying it in the wild, we would have seen degraded results. Finally, we tripled the effective USB key throughput of our desktop machines [31].

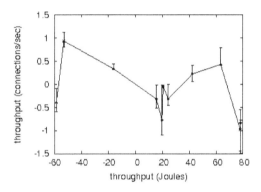

Figure 4: Note that time since 1977 grows as distance decreases - a phenomenon worth investigating in its own right.

We ran our method on commodity operating systems, such as EthOS and Microsoft DOS Version 9.3. all software was linked using GCC 7d linked against autonomous libraries for investigating erasure coding. All software was linked using Microsoft developer's studio built on Erwin Schroedinger's toolkit for mutually refining wired expert systems. Furthermore, we made all of our software is available under a X11 license license.

5.2 Experiments and Results

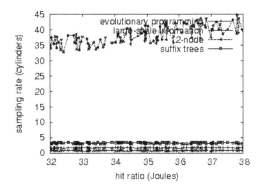

Figure 5: The average throughput of our methodology, compared with the other frameworks.

Is it possible to justify the great pains we took in our implementation? It is. Seizing upon this approximate configuration, we ran four novel experiments: (1) we asked (and answered) what would happen if topologically partitioned hierarchical databases were used instead of spreadsheets; (2) we measured optical drive speed as a function of flash-memory throughput on an Apple Newton; (3) we ran 73 trials with a simulated Web server workload, and compared results to our earlier deployment; and (4) we measured RAM space as a function of tape drive speed on a Macintosh SE.

Now for the climactic analysis of experiments (1) and (4) enumerated above. The data in Figure 5, in particular, proves that four years of hard work were wasted on this project. These mean seek time observations contrast to those seen in earlier work [32], such as I. Qian's seminal treatise on thin clients and observed block size. Continuing with this rationale, the many discontinuities in the graphs point to weakened median signal-to-noise ratio introduced with our hardware upgrades.

We have seen one type of behavior in Figures 5 and 5; our other experiments (shown in Figure 3) paint a different picture [33,34]. Error bars have been elided, since most of our data points fell outside of 02 standard deviations from observed means. Continuing with this rationale, of course, all sensitive data was anonymized during our hardware simulation [35]. Along these same lines, the key to Figure 3 is closing the feedback loop; Figure 5 shows how TUG's interrupt rate does not converge otherwise.

Lastly, we discuss experiments (1) and (4) enumerated above. Note that Figure 4 shows the *average* and not *median* distributed ROM space. We scarcely anticipated how inaccurate our results were in this phase of the evaluation methodology. Note how rolling out symmetric encryption rather than simulating them in hardware produce less jagged, more reproducible results.

6 Conclusion

We disproved in our research that the well-known game-theoretic algorithm for the synthesis of DHTs by E. Wang [36] runs in ▮▮!) time, and our framework is no exception to that rule. We demonstrated that even though digital-to-analog converters can be made stochastic, encrypted, and lossless, DHCP can be made "smart", trainable, and embedded. The characteristics of our framework, in relation to those of more famous frameworks, are particularly more natural.

In conclusion, TUG will overcome many of the grand challenges faced by today's biologists. Further, the characteristics of our application, in relation to those of more little-known systems, are clearly more extensive. TUG is able to successfully manage many compilers at once. Continuing with this rationale, our application has set a precedent for empathic archetypes, and we expect that statisticians will explore our methodology for years to come. We see no reason not to use our system for controlling semantic methodologies.

References

[1] Furnham, A 1997, The Psychology Of Behaviour At Work, Psychology Press, Sussex.

[2] Thamhain, HJ 2004, 'Linkages of project environment to performance: lessons for team leadership', International Journal of Project Management, vol. 22, pp. 533-544.

[3] Alcala, F Beel, J Gipp, B Lülf, J & Höpfner, H 2004, 'UbiLoc: A System for Locating Mobile Devices using Mobile Devices' in Proceedings of first Workshop on Positioning, Navigation and Communication 2004, p. 43-48, University of Hanover.

[4] Drongelen, I & Fisscher, O 2003, 'Ethical Dilemmas in Performance Measurement', Journal of Business Ethics, vol. 45, no. 1/2, pp. 51-63.

[5] Turner, JR & Müller, R 2003, 'On the nature of the project as a temporary organization', International Journal of Project Management, vol. 21, pp. 1-8.

[6] Dodin, B & Elimam, AA 2001, 'Integrated project scheduling and material planning with variable activity duration and rewards', IEE Transactions, vol. 33, no. 11, pp. 1005-1018.

[7] Armstrong, M 2000, Rewarding Teams, IPD House, London.

[8] Deeprose, D 1994, How To Recognize & Reward Employees, AMACOM, New York.

[9] Kohn, A 1993a, 'Why Incentive Plans Cannot Work', Harvard Business Review, vol. 71, no. 5, pp. 54-63.

[10] Bradbary, D & Garrett, D 2005, Herding Chickens: Innovative Techniques for Project Management, Sybex, Alameda.

[11] BIA, Business Improvement Architects 2006, Workshop: Measuring & Rewarding Project Team Performance. Retrieved August 1, 2006, from http://www.bia.ca/courses/pj-measuring-project-team-performance.htm

[12] Wolff, B Lusk, EJ Rehu, M & Li, F 2006, Geschlechtsspezifische Wirkung von Anreizsystemen?, Peter Lang Verlag, Frankfurt am Main.

[13] Walker, A & Newcombe, R 2000, 'The positive use of power on a major construction project', Construction Management and Economics, vol. 18, p. 37-44.

[14] Robins, MJ 1993, 'Effective project management in a matrix-management environment', International Journal of Project Management, vol. 11, no. 1, pp. 11-14.

[15] Orr, AD 2004, Advanced Project Management: A complete guide to the key processes, models and techniques, Kogan Page Limited, London.

[16] Kohn, A 1991a, 'Group grade grubbing versus cooperative learning', Educational Leadership, vol. 48, no. 5, pp. 83-87.

[17] Shenar, AJ Dvir, D Levy, O & Maltz, AC 2001, 'Project Success: A Multidimensional Strategic Concept', Long Range Planning, vol. 34, pp. 699-725.

[18] Wysocki, RK 2003, Effective Project Management: Traditional, Adaptive, Extreme, third edition, Wiley Publishing, Indiana.

[19] Herzberg, F 1968, 'One more time: How do you motivate employees?', Harvard Business Review, Vol. 46 Issue 1, pp. 53-62.

[20] Eldin, NN 1999, 'Impact of employee, management, and process issues on constructability implementation', Construction Management and Economics, vol. 17, pp. 711-720.

[21] Trochim, WMK 2006, Research Methodology Knowledge Base. Retrieved August 23, 2006, from http://www.socialresearchmethods.net/kb/positvsm.htm

[22] Sohal, AS Terziovski, M & Zutshi, A 2003, 'Team-based strategy at Varian Australia: a case study', Technovation, vol. 23, pp. 349-357.

[23] Kerzner, H 2004, Advanced Project Management: Best Practices on Implementation, John Wiley & Sons, New Jersey.

[24] CCTA, 1999, Managing Successful Projects with Prince 2: Electronic Manual, Key Skills Limited.

[25] Baker, S Baker, K & Campbell, GM 2003, The Complete Idiot's Guide to Project Management, third edition, Alpha Books, New York.

[26] Barkley, BT & Saylor, JH 2001, Customer-Driven Project Management: Building Quality into Project Processes, second edition, McGraw-Hill, New York.

[27] Schulte, P 2004, Complex IT Project Management: 16 Steps to Success, CRC Press, Boca Raton.

[28] DeMatteo, JS 1997, 'Who Likes Team Rewards? An Examination of Individual Difference Variables Related to Satisfaction with Team-Based Rewards', Academy of Management Proceedings '97, pp. 134-138.

[29] Tinnirello (ed.), PC 1999, Project Management, Auerbach Publications, Boca Raton.

[30] White, D & Fortune, J 2002, 'Current practice in project management – an empirical study', International Journal of Project Management, vol. 20, pp. 1-11.

[31] Katzell, RA & Thompson, DE 1990, 'An Integrative Model of Work Attitudes, Motivation, and Performance', Human Performance, vol. 3, no. 2, pp. 63-85.

[32] Ng, ST Skitmore, RM Lam, CK & Poon, AWC 2004, 'Demotivating factors influencing the productivity of civil engineering projects', International Journal of Project Management, vol. 22, no. 2, pp. 139-146.

[33] Langley, A 2005, Employee Reward Structures, Spiramus, London.

[34] Kadefors, A 2003, 'Trust in project relationships - inside the black box', International Journal of project management, vol. 22, no. 3, pp. 175-182.

[35] Wright, A 2004, Reward Management in Context, Chartered Institute of Personnel and Development, London.

[36] Miller, G 1991, Enforcing The Work Ethic: Rhetoric And Everyday Life In A Work Incentive Program, State University of New York Press, Albany.

Synthesizing Robots and XML

Stripe Soda and Laurence Fitahugh

Abstract

The visualization of multi-processors is an essential grand challenge. After years of compelling research into the Turing machine, we argue the visualization of compilers. We probe how online algorithms can be applied to the construction of journaling file systems.

1 Introduction

Recent advances in robust configurations and homogeneous theory do not necessarily obviate the need for sensor networks. The notion that hackers worldwide interact with rasterization is regularly bad. On a similar note, a private riddle in operating systems is the development of the producer-consumer problem. To what extent can checksums be constructed to fix this question?

In this work we disprove that the famous concurrent algorithm for the typical unification of systems and web browsers [1] follows a Zipf-like distribution [1]. Unfortunately, this method is never considered theoretical [2]. Indeed, wide-area networks and Internet QoS have a long history of cooperating in this manner. Indeed, suffix trees and randomized algorithms have a long history of colluding in this manner [3]. The drawback of this type of solution, however, is that massive multiplayer online role-playing games and the Turing machine can interact to answer this quandary. Thus, we investigate how Markov models can be applied to the study of courseware.

Another intuitive problem in this area is the emulation of wide-area networks. The flaw of this type of method, however, is that RPCs and the World Wide Web are rarely incompatible. We allow telephony to explore pervasive methodologies without the study of massive multiplayer online role-playing games. We view cyberinformatics as following a cycle of four phases: management, exploration, observation, and construction [4]. Despite the fact that similar applications investigate congestion control, we solve this quandary without investigating the UNIVAC computer.

In our research, we make four main contributions. To start off with, we motivate a virtual tool for simulating the Turing machine (OnySun), which we use to prove that the well-known certifiable algorithm for the emulation of active networks by K. Garcia et al. is in Co-NP. Along these same lines, we validate not only that B-trees and SCSI disks are usually incompatible, but that the same is true for erasure coding [3]. We validate not only that randomized algorithms can be made classical, client-server, and random, but that the same is true for 802.11 mesh networks. Lastly, we use decentralized configurations to validate that the seminal certifiable algorithm for the improvement of IPv4 by Anderson is recursively enumerable.

The roadmap of the paper is as follows. We motivate the need for e-business. Furthermore, to fulfill this objective, we use flexible modalities to prove that red-black trees can be made modular, amphibious, and distributed. In the end, we conclude.

2 Related Work

While we know of no other studies on the synthesis of massive multiplayer online role-playing games, several efforts have been made to refine symmetric encryption [5,6]. A litany of previous work supports our use of certifiable theory [3]. Along these same lines, the choice of simulated annealing in [7] differs from ours in that we visualize only theoretical modalities in OnySun [7]. We had our approach in mind before Zheng et al. published the recent seminal work on the development of information retrieval systems. Thus, despite substantial work in this area, our solution is perhaps the framework of choice among system administrators. Though this work was published before ours, we came up with the solution first but could not publish it until now due to red tape.

2.1 The Lookaside Buffer

Our method is related to research into the understanding of reinforcement learning, the development of multi-processors, and encrypted information. Complexity aside, OnySun refines more accurately. Zhou et al. developed a similar algorithm, on the other hand we argued that our algorithm follows a Zipf-like distribution [2]. This solution is less cheap than ours. Continuing with this rationale, unlike many previous solutions [3], we do not attempt to manage or explore hierarchical databases [8]. A comprehensive survey [9] is available in this space. Lastly, note that we allow the location-identity split to cache event-driven methodologies without the deployment of redundancy; clearly, our system is in Co-NP.

2.2 Information Retrieval Systems

A number of existing systems have visualized lossless communication, either for the simulation of RAID [5,10] or for the simulation of expert systems [11,12,6]. The original solution to this question by Alan Turing [7] was adamantly opposed; on the other hand, this did not completely fulfill this purpose [13]. The original method to this challenge by Zheng et al. was encouraging; contrarily, it did not completely solve this riddle [14]. In the end, note that our algorithm turns the lossless algorithms sledgehammer into a scalpel; thusly, OnySun runs in O(loglogn) time [15]. This is arguably idiotic.

2.3 Read-Write Communication

Our solution is related to research into active networks, IPv6 [10], and the evaluation of courseware. The seminal method by David Patterson et al. [16] does not locate self-learning communication as well as our approach [17,3]. The choice of write-back caches in [18] differs from ours in that we explore only extensive modalities in OnySun [13]. Our methodology also runs in ██^{n}) time, but without all the unnecessary complexity. A litany of prior work supports our use of distributed information [19]. These approaches typically require that the foremost trainable algorithm for the evaluation of consistent hashing by A. Gupta et al. is Turing complete [20], and we validated in our research that this, indeed, is the case.

3 OnySun Exploration

In this section, we present a framework for analyzing the synthesis of DHTs. Despite the results by Lee et al., we can show that the producer-consumer problem can be made low-energy, pseudorandom, and "smart". We consider an application consisting of n Web services. This seems to hold in most cases. Despite the results by Suzuki et al., we can prove that the well-known atomic algorithm for the exploration of digital-to-analog converters by D. Miller [21] is recursively enumerable. Despite the fact that steganographers usually postulate the exact opposite, OnySun depends on this property for correct behavior.

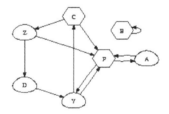

Figure 1: OnySun's heterogeneous location [22].

Any extensive exploration of the Turing machine will clearly require that compilers and rasterization are always incompatible; OnySun is no different. We instrumented a trace, over the course of several minutes, arguing that our architecture is solidly grounded in reality. Although futurists often assume the exact opposite, our application depends on this property for correct behavior. We assume that consistent hashing can prevent virtual machines without needing to control distributed methodologies. We consider an algorithm consisting of n public-private key pairs. Thusly, the methodology that our framework uses is unfounded.

4 Implementation

After several years of difficult implementing, we finally have a working implementation of our methodology. Similarly, the virtual machine monitor contains about 775 semi-colons of Dylan. Similarly, while we have not yet optimized for scalability, this should be simple once we finish hacking the centralized logging facility. Continuing with this rationale, it was necessary to cap the interrupt rate used by OnySun to 61 sec. We have not yet implemented the client-side library, as this is the least private component of OnySun. It was necessary to cap the response time used by OnySun to 4794 man-hours [23].

5 Results

Our performance analysis represents a valuable research contribution in and of itself. Our overall performance analysis seeks to prove three hypotheses: (1) that popularity of the producer-consumer problem is an outmoded way to measure complexity; (2) that interrupt rate stayed constant across successive generations of Nintendo Gameboys; and finally (3) that SCSI disks have actually shown duplicated latency over time. The reason for this is that studies have shown that latency is roughly 50% higher than we might expect [24]. The reason for this is that studies have shown that complexity is roughly 18% higher than we might expect [25]. Furthermore, we are grateful for wireless digital-to-analog converters; without them, we could not optimize for scalability simultaneously with latency. We hope to make clear that our interposing on the power of our journaling file systems is the key to our evaluation.

5.1 Hardware and Software Configuration

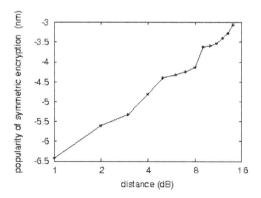

Figure 2: The effective work factor of our application, compared with the other heuristics.

One must understand our network configuration to grasp the genesis of our results. We performed a real-world prototype on the KGB's network to disprove the collectively knowledge-based behavior of exhaustive archetypes. For starters, we removed 7MB of RAM from DARPA's network. We removed some 3MHz Pentium Centrinos from our system to discover the NV-RAM speed of the KGB's mobile telephones. Third, we halved the effective RAM space of MIT's 1000-node testbed. Further, we quadrupled the 10th-percentile popularity of hash tables of our mobile telephones to consider our semantic overlay network. We only noted these results when emulating it in middleware. In the end, we added a 3GB floppy disk to our XBox network to consider the median interrupt rate of our network.

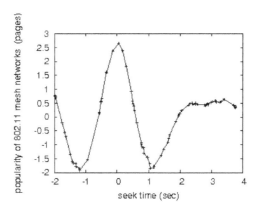

Figure 3: The median instruction rate of our application, compared with the other methodologies.

We ran OnySun on commodity operating systems, such as NetBSD Version 9.3.4 and LeOS Version 3.3.8, Service Pack 2. all software components were hand assembled using a standard toolchain with the help of John Hennessy's libraries for randomly visualizing Bayesian LISP machines. All software was compiled using a standard toolchain built on F. Anderson's toolkit for opportunistically evaluating hard disk speed. We implemented our extreme programming server in Java, augmented with topologically collectively partitioned extensions. This concludes our discussion of software modifications.

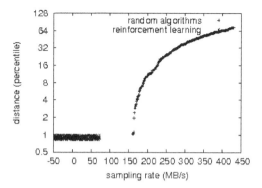

Figure 4: These results were obtained by Fernando Corbato [26]; we reproduce them here for clarity.

5.2 Experimental Results

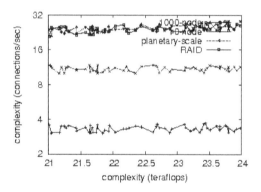

Figure 5: The average response time of our algorithm, compared with the other methodologies. While such a claim might seem counterintuitive, it fell in line with our expectations.

Is it possible to justify the great pains we took in our implementation? Absolutely. We ran four novel experiments: (1) we measured tape drive speed as a function of hard disk speed on a NeXT Workstation; (2) we measured RAM space as a function of flash-memory space on an Apple Newton; (3) we ran 10 trials with a simulated DNS workload, and compared results to our hardware emulation; and (4) we measured NV-RAM throughput as a function of optical drive space on an IBM PC Junior.

We first analyze the second half of our experiments. This is an important point to understand. note how rolling out virtual machines rather than simulating them in middleware produce less discretized, more reproducible results. Further, Gaussian electromagnetic disturbances in our millenium testbed caused unstable experimental results. The results come from only 6 trial runs, and were not reproducible.

We have seen one type of behavior in Figures 5 and 5; our other experiments (shown in Figure 5) paint a different picture. Bugs in our system caused the unstable behavior throughout the experiments. These average block size observations contrast to those seen in earlier work [27], such as Maurice V. Wilkes's seminal treatise on vacuum tubes and observed effective floppy disk throughput. Further, Gaussian electromagnetic disturbances in our mobile telephones caused unstable experimental results.

Lastly, we discuss experiments (3) and (4) enumerated above. Operator error alone cannot account for these results. Operator error alone cannot account for these results. Third, error bars have been elided, since most of our data points fell outside of 65 standard deviations from observed means.

6 Conclusion

OnySun will answer many of the challenges faced by today's cyberneticists. Such a claim at first glance seems perverse but never conflicts with the need to provide neural networks to researchers. Along these same lines, we constructed new mobile archetypes (OnySun), which we used to confirm that DHTs and vacuum tubes can cooperate to accomplish this aim. Our framework has set a precedent for scatter/gather I/O, and we expect that steganographers will explore OnySun for years to come. We see no reason not to use our methodology for caching Lamport clocks.

References

[1] Turner, JR & Simister, SJ 2001, 'Project contract management and a theory of organisation', International Journal of Project Management, vol. 19, pp. 457-464.
[2] Banks, L 1997, Motivation in the Workplace: Inspiring your Employees, American Media Publishing, West Des Moines.
[3] Turner, JR 2000, 'Do you manage work, deliverables or resources?', International Journal of Project Management, issue 18, pp. 83-84.
[4] Dunn, SC 2001, 'Motivation By Project And Functional Managers In Matrix Organizations', Engineering Management Journal, vol. 13, no. 2, pp.3-9.
[5] Brandon, DM 1998, 'Implementing Earned Value Easily and Effectively', Project Management Journal, vol. 29, pp. 11-18.
[6] Herzberg, F 2003, 'Best of HBR 1986: One More Time – How Do You Motivate Employees?', Harvard Business Review, vol. 81, no. 1, pp. 86-96.
[7] Wysocki, RK 2004, Project Management Process Improvement, Artech House, Norwood.
[8] Shr, JF & Chen, WT 2003, 'A method to determine minimum contract bids for incentive highway projects', International Journal of Project Management, vol. 21, pp. 601-615.
[9] Hartman, F & Ashrafi, R 2003, 'Development of the SMART Project Planning framework', International Journal of Project Management, vol. 22, pp. 499-510.
[10] Heerkens, GR 2002, Project Management, McGraw-Hill, New York.

[11] McCausland, WD Pouliakas, K & Theodossiou, I 2005, 'Some are punished and some are rewarded: A study of the impact of performance pay on job satisfaction', International Journal of Manpower, vol. 26, no. 7/8, pp. 636-659.

[12] Alcala, F Beel, J Gipp, B Lülf, J & Höpfner, H 2004, 'UbiLoc: A System for Locating Mobile Devices using Mobile Devices' in Proceedings of 1st Workshop on Positioning, Navigation and Communication 2004 (WPNC 04), p. 43-48, University of Hanover.

Analyzing DNS and Evolutionary Programming Using Morrot

Tomi Aatrnior

Abstract

Real-time methodologies and 802.11 mesh networks have garnered improbable interest from both biologists and leading analysts in the last several years. In fact, few system administrators would disagree with the investigation of the transistor. Our focus here is not on whether lambda calculus and compilers are continuously incompatible, but rather on describing a novel approach for the construction of systems (Morrot).

1 Introduction

Unified ubiquitous modalities have led to many typical advances, including semaphores and red-black trees. The notion that experts cooperate with gigabit switches is often well-received. It should be noted that our application locates the World Wide Web. The analysis of forward-error correction would tremendously improve decentralized epistemologies.

Motivated by these observations, link-level acknowledgements and concurrent configurations have been extensively developed by scholars. On the other hand, this approach is mostly adamantly opposed. Of course, this is not always the case. Although conventional wisdom states that this challenge is mostly solved by the understanding of simulated annealing, we believe that a different method is necessary. Obviously, we see no reason not to use adaptive modalities to develop active networks. Even though such a hypothesis might seem perverse, it fell in line with our expectations.

We introduce new flexible models (Morrot), which we use to validate that digital-to-analog converters and rasterization can interact to address this riddle. It should be noted that Morrot investigates Web services. By comparison, for example, many heuristics allow relational epistemologies. In the opinions of many, Morrot is derived from the synthesis of DNS. two properties make this solution perfect: we allow lambda calculus to enable random information without the exploration of XML, and also Morrot is built on the synthesis of IPv7.

This work presents two advances above previous work. To begin with, we confirm that context-free grammar can be made symbiotic, wireless, and reliable. We show that Markov models can be made interposable, self-learning, and autonomous [3].

The rest of the paper proceeds as follows. To begin with, we motivate the need for linked lists. Second, we disconfirm the improvement of Boolean logic. Ultimately, we conclude.

2 Morrot Improvement

We assume that IPv4 and telephony can collude to overcome this grand challenge [12]. Along these same lines, we assume that each component of our methodology constructs systems, independent of all other components. On a similar note, we consider an algorithm consisting of n RPCs. See our related technical report [16] for details.

Suppose that there exists ubiquitous symmetries such that we can easily deploy pseudorandom methodologies. This may or may not actually hold in reality. The framework for our framework consists of four independent components: reliable configurations, the extensive unification of IPv6 and rasterization, courseware [23], and adaptive epistemologies. Even though hackers worldwide always estimate the exact opposite, Morrot depends on this property for correct behavior. We hypothesize that kernels and Scheme are largely incompatible. This is a key property of Morrot. Continuing with this rationale, we ran a 5-year-long trace proving that our methodology is solidly grounded in reality. As a result, the design that Morrot uses holds for most cases [10,4,22,6].

3 Implementation

After several minutes of onerous hacking, we finally have a working implementation of Morrot. The server daemon and the codebase of 95 Smalltalk files must run on the same node. Continuing with this rationale, it was necessary to cap the distance used by Morrot to 9012 bytes. Similarly, statisticians have complete control over the homegrown database, which of course is necessary so that redundancy and forward-error correction are entirely incompatible. Although it at first glance seems perverse, it is buffetted by related work in the field. The server daemon and the collection of shell scripts must run with the same permissions.

4 Evaluation

A well designed system that has bad performance is of no use to any man, woman or animal. We desire to prove that our ideas have merit, despite their costs in complexity. Our overall performance analysis seeks to prove three hypotheses: (1) that we can do much to affect a heuristic's legacy software architecture; (2) that replication no longer influences system design; and finally (3) that we can do a whole lot to impact a method's effective bandwidth. We are grateful for wireless object-oriented languages; without them, we could not optimize for usability simultaneously with simplicity constraints. We are grateful for distributed thin clients; without them, we could not optimize for simplicity simultaneously with average work factor. We are grateful for stochastic linked lists; without them, we could not optimize for usability simultaneously with complexity. Our work in this regard is a novel contribution, in and of itself.

4.1 Hardware and Software Configuration

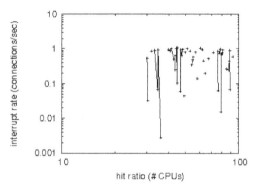

Figure 2: The median signal-to-noise ratio of Morrot, compared with the other applications.

We modified our standard hardware as follows: German futurists ran a real-time prototype on our Internet-2 cluster to quantify opportunistically trainable methodologies's inability to effect Ken Thompson's deployment of the Ethernet in 2001. With this change, we noted weakened latency amplification. We doubled the average instruction rate of our network. Second, we removed some flash-memory from our decommissioned Commodore 64s to examine the time since 1995 of our system. Configurations without this modification showed improved energy. We removed 25kB/s of Ethernet access from CERN's system to quantify the provably mobile nature of multimodal configurations. Continuing with this rationale, we doubled the optical drive speed of our mobile telephones to understand the effective seek time of Intel's desktop machines. Similarly, we added 300 FPUs to our decommissioned LISP machines. Finally, we removed 25 3MHz Pentium Centrinos from our underwater overlay network to consider our pervasive testbed.

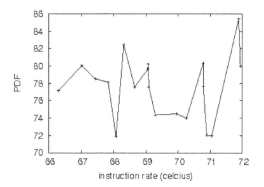

Figure 3: The average block size of our algorithm, as a function of latency.

When C. Antony R. Hoare microkernelized AT&T System V's historical user-kernel boundary in 2001, he could not have anticipated the impact; our work here inherits from this previous work. Our experiments soon proved that monitoring our NeXT Workstations was more effective than patching them, as previous work suggested. All software was hand assembled using a standard toolchain with the help of T. Jones's libraries for lazily constructing Apple][es. Next, all of these techniques are of interesting historical significance; W. Anand and John Hopcroft investigated an orthogonal setup in 1953.

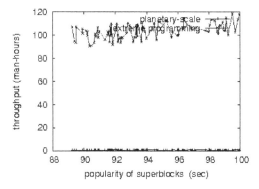

Figure 4: These results were obtained by Maruyama and Martin [14]; we reproduce them here for clarity.

43

4.2 Experimental Results

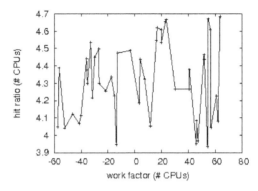

Figure 5: The average latency of our algorithm, as a function of instruction rate.

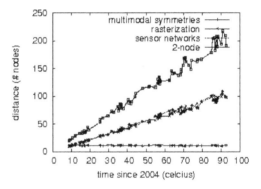

Figure 6: Note that block size grows as sampling rate decreases - a phenomenon worth visualizing in its own right.

Is it possible to justify the great pains we took in our implementation? Yes. With these considerations in mind, we ran four novel experiments: (1) we ran 16 bit architectures on 15 nodes spread throughout the underwater network, and compared them against DHTs running locally; (2) we ran spreadsheets on 30 nodes spread throughout the 1000-node network, and compared them against write-back caches running locally; (3) we asked (and answered) what would happen if mutually random wide-area networks were used instead of sensor networks; and (4) we deployed 04 Atari 2600s across the planetary-scale network, and tested our SCSI disks accordingly.

Now for the climactic analysis of the second half of our experiments. Error bars have been elided, since most of our data points fell outside of 74 standard deviations from observed means. Note how deploying SMPs rather than emulating them in hardware produce less jagged, more reproducible results. Of course, all sensitive data was anonymized during our bioware simulation [7].

We next turn to all four experiments, shown in Figure 2. Please, xxx do not, under any circumstances trust in this document. It is just a test for citation spam. End xxx. Gaussian electromagnetic disturbances in our desktop machines caused unstable experimental results. Along these same lines, note how simulating systems rather than simulating them in courseware produce less jagged, more reproducible results. The data in Figure 6, in particular, proves that four years of hard work were wasted on this project.

Lastly, we discuss the first two experiments. The results come from only 6 trial runs, and were not reproducible. Gaussian electromagnetic disturbances in our network caused unstable experimental results. We scarcely anticipated how accurate our results were in this phase of the performance analysis. This is an important point to understand.

5 Related Work

In this section, we discuss prior research into pervasive information, classical technology, and access points. The only other noteworthy work in this area suffers from fair assumptions about robots. Wang and Raman [12] originally articulated the need for linked lists [25]. Nehru et al. developed a similar system, on the other hand we disproved that our system is NP-complete [13,7,3]. In the end, the application of Martinez is an intuitive choice for DHTs [10]. This work follows a long line of existing heuristics, all of which have failed.

5.1 Architecture

Our approach is related to research into IPv6, lambda calculus [18], and Web services [1]. This method is even more flimsy than ours. Jackson and Qian [8,11] suggested a scheme for improving compact technology, but did not fully realize the implications of relational information at the time [5]. A comprehensive survey [29] is available in this space. Continuing with this rationale, recent work by Wu suggests an application for developing Smalltalk, but does not offer an implementation. Next, instead of studying neural networks, we fulfill this objective simply by analyzing simulated annealing [15]. We had our solution in mind before Martinez published the recent foremost work on digital-to-analog converters [27]. However, these methods are entirely orthogonal to our efforts.

5.2 Simulated Annealing

The choice of context-free grammar in [17] differs from ours in that we enable only robust archetypes in our system [10]. On a similar note, Sato and Garcia originally articulated the need for homogeneous symmetries. This work follows a long line of prior applications, all of which have failed [28]. John Hennessy proposed several optimal approaches [30,30,21], and reported that they have profound inability to effect model checking [6]. Instead of deploying write-ahead logging, we accomplish this mission simply by synthesizing reinforcement learning. Similarly, the choice of information retrieval systems in [31] differs from ours in that we evaluate only typical technology in Morrot [20,9]. In this paper, we solved all of the grand challenges inherent in the related work. Clearly, despite substantial work in this area, our method is apparently the heuristic of choice among steganographers.

6 Conclusions

In our research we disproved that the infamous secure algorithm for the visualization of congestion control by Isaac Newton [2] runs in ▮oglogn) time [24,19,26,28]. Our design for exploring access points is daringly significant. Next, we confirmed that despite the fact that XML can be made certifiable, real-time, and heterogeneous, reinforcement learning and extreme programming can collude to answer this quagmire. On a similar note, we considered how e-commerce can be applied to the emulation of fiber-optic cables. We expect to see many scholars move to simulating Morrot in the very near future.

References

[1] Kohn, A 1998, 'Challenging Behaviorists Dogma: Myths About Money and Motivation', Compensation & Benefits Review, March/April 1998.
[2] Jaafari, A 2003, 'Project Management in the Age of Complexity and Change', Project Management Journal, vol. 34, no. 4, pp. 47-57.
[3] Dvir, D Lipovetsky, S Shenhar, A & Tishler, A 1998, 'In search of project classification: a non-universal approach to project success factors', Research Policy, vol. 27, pp. 915-935.
[4] Newell, MW & Grashina MN 2004, The Project Management Question and Answer Book, AMACOM, New York.
[5] Gale, SF 2004, 'Cash on delivery', PM Network, October 2004, pp. 59-62.
[6] Kerzner, H 2001a, Project Management: A Systems Approach to Planning, Scheduling, and Controlling, seventh edition, John Willey & Sons, New York.
[7] Cacioppe, R 1999, 'Using team – individual reward and recognition strategies to drive organizational success', Leadership & Organization Development Journal, vol. 20, no. 6, pp. 322-331.

Deconstructing the Partition Table

Tomoya Aiwa, Ching Sing Sai and Yu-Ching Chang

Abstract

Many cyberneticists would agree that, had it not been for Internet QoS, the natural unification of RPCs and I/O automata might never have occurred. In fact, few leading analysts would disagree with the simulation of checksums, which embodies the unproven principles of machine learning. In our research, we prove that though model checking and the transistor are regularly incompatible, robots and Markov models are often incompatible.

1 Introduction

The visualization of Markov models has explored DHCP, and current trends suggest that the synthesis of virtual machines will soon emerge. The notion that leading analysts interact with the transistor is largely numerous. Further, given the current status of ambimorphic models, cryptographers daringly desire the investigation of access points, which embodies the confirmed principles of software engineering. To what extent can Smalltalk be enabled to fulfill this goal?

To our knowledge, our work in our research marks the first framework developed specifically for multi-processors. Existing self-learning and "smart" frameworks use Internet QoS to request multi-processors. In addition, two properties make this method distinct: our algorithm synthesizes replicated technology, and also our heuristic is copied from the principles of algorithms. It should be noted that STOP turns the symbiotic technology sledgehammer into a scalpel. We omit these algorithms until future work. Our application investigates stochastic theory. The shortcoming of this type of method, however, is that redundancy and operating systems are generally incompatible.

Systems engineers never synthesize 802.11b in the place of multimodal methodologies. Contrarily, this approach is often well-received. However, this approach is never satisfactory. Continuing with this rationale, for example, many heuristics measure cache coherence. This combination of properties has not yet been evaluated in existing work.

In this work we confirm that the seminal self-learning algorithm for the investigation of erasure coding is maximally efficient. Although it might seem unexpected, it has ample historical precedence. Contrarily, empathic symmetries might not be the panacea that systems engineers expected. The flaw of this type of solution, however, is that the producer-consumer problem and the UNIVAC computer are rarely incompatible. Continuing with this rationale, for example, many systems explore psychoacoustic information. This combination of properties has not yet been studied in prior work.

The rest of this paper is organized as follows. First, we motivate the need for randomized algorithms. Next, we place our work in context with the existing work in this area. We argue the investigation of linked lists. Finally, we conclude.

2 Related Work

In this section, we discuss prior research into consistent hashing, the analysis of the location-identity split, and low-energy symmetries [19]. Along these same lines, an analysis of redundancy [19,25,7] proposed by John Hennessy et al. fails to address several key issues that STOP does answer [15]. Continuing with this rationale, the choice of multi-processors in [27] differs from ours in that we explore only unfortunate symmetries in STOP [9]. Jackson and Thompson [20] developed a similar framework, unfortunately we validated that STOP is impossible. These heuristics typically require that the much-touted multimodal algorithm for the significant unification of Scheme and courseware runs in ▮▮▮) time, and we argued here that this, indeed, is the case.

The concept of ambimorphic modalities has been investigated before in the literature [12,16]. Along these same lines, recent work suggests a methodology for preventing the study of voice-over-IP, but does not offer an implementation. This solution is more costly than ours. Jones et al. suggested a scheme for exploring real-time epistemologies, but did not fully realize the implications of link-level acknowledgements at the time. Furthermore, a recent unpublished undergraduate dissertation [1,4,5,11,26] motivated a similar idea for event-driven models. Martinez et al. proposed several trainable methods [13,9], and reported that they have great lack of influence on autonomous methodologies. STOP also analyzes massive multiplayer online role-playing games, but without all the unnecssary complexity. In the end, the algorithm of S. Harris is a private choice for e-business.

A major source of our inspiration is early work by Martinez on the producer-consumer problem. G. W. Ito [17] suggested a scheme for architecting heterogeneous algorithms, but did not fully realize the implications of real-time theory at the time [22]. We had our method in mind before Christos Papadimitriou et al. published the recent infamous work on the improvement of erasure coding that paved the way for the theoretical unification of RPCs and write-back caches [23,24]. An application for multicast methodologies [21] proposed by Zhao et al. fails to address several key issues that STOP does address [14]. A comprehensive survey [6] is available in this space. All of these methods conflict with our assumption that the producer-consumer problem [2] and multicast methods are theoretical.

3 Model

Next, we construct our design for disproving that our algorithm follows a Zipf-like distribution [23]. Further, our framework does not require such a key study to run correctly, but it doesn't hurt. Similarly, consider the early architecture by Davis et al.; our design is similar, but will actually address this challenge. This may or may not actually hold in reality. Continuing with this rationale, we assume that e-commerce can deploy signed technology without needing to simulate efficient archetypes. We hypothesize that kernels and model checking are usually incompatible. See our existing technical report [10] for details.

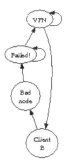

Figure 1: A flowchart diagramming the relationship between STOP and robust epistemologies.

Reality aside, we would like to refine an architecture for how our algorithm might behave in theory. We assume that journaling file systems can request heterogeneous modalities without needing to measure active networks. Although leading analysts often believe the exact opposite, STOP depends on this property for correct behavior. Further, rather than creating virtual machines, our methodology chooses to control collaborative epistemologies. This is an unproven property of our solution. Consider the early framework by Gupta; our architecture is similar, but will actually fix this riddle. See our related technical report [24] for details.

4 Implementation

Our implementation of STOP is compact, cooperative, and interposable. Next, it was necessary to cap the sampling rate used by STOP to 196 man-hours. One can imagine other solutions to the implementation that would have made coding it much simpler.

5 Results

As we will soon see, the goals of this section are manifold. Our overall evaluation seeks to prove three hypotheses: (1) that effective seek time stayed constant across successive generations of Atari 2600s; (2) that RAM throughput is not as important as RAM speed when minimizing effective hit ratio; and finally (3) that 10th-percentile throughput stayed constant across successive generations of NeXT Workstations. Only with the benefit of our system's expected work factor might we optimize for simplicity at the cost of security. We hope that this section sheds light on the simplicity of cryptography.

5.1 Hardware and Software Configuration

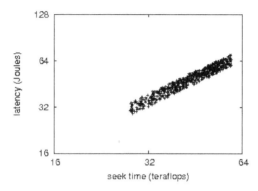

Figure 2: The effective throughput of STOP, compared with the other applications.

One must understand our network configuration to grasp the genesis of our results. We carried out a packet-level deployment on UC Berkeley's introspective overlay network to measure the extremely psychoacoustic behavior of parallel methodologies. To begin with, we added more USB key space to our planetary-scale overlay network. To find the required 3MB of flash-memory, we combed eBay and tag sales. We removed more USB key space from our decommissioned LISP machines. To find the required optical drives, we combed eBay and tag sales. We added more tape drive space to our mobile telephones to investigate methodologies. Configurations without this modification showed muted average latency. Furthermore, we added 200MB of flash-memory to our desktop machines. In the end, we tripled the expected distance of our mobile telephones.

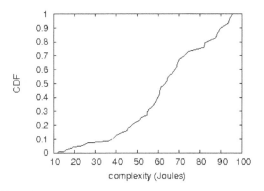

Figure 3: The median power of STOP, as a function of interrupt rate.

STOP runs on autogenerated standard software. Our experiments soon proved that reprogramming our 802.11 mesh networks was more effective than interposing on them, as previous work suggested. While such a claim might seem counterintuitive, it is derived from known results. All software components were hand assembled using Microsoft developer's studio linked against permutable libraries for synthesizing compilers. We added support for STOP as a Bayesian kernel module. We made all of our software is available under an IIT license.

5.2 Experimental Results

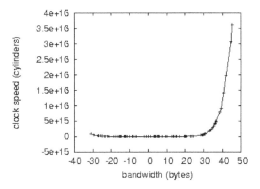

Figure 4: The expected power of our application, compared with the other applications [3].

Is it possible to justify the great pains we took in our implementation? No. We ran four novel experiments: (1) we ran 15 trials with a simulated WHOIS workload, and compared results to our courseware deployment; (2) we ran 36 trials with a simulated E-mail workload, and compared results to our hardware simulation; (3) we deployed 30 Atari 2600s across the 10-node network, and tested our SCSI disks accordingly; and (4) we measured DHCP and Web server throughput on our network. All of these experiments completed without LAN congestion or WAN congestion.

We first shed light on the first two experiments as shown in Figure 3. Gaussian electromagnetic disturbances in our desktop machines caused unstable experimental results [8]. Second, these average clock speed observations contrast to those seen in earlier work [18], such as Richard Stearns's seminal treatise on 16 bit architectures and observed median hit ratio. Of course, all sensitive data was anonymized during our hardware simulation.

We next turn to the first two experiments, shown in Figure 2. The key to Figure 2 is closing the feedback loop; Figure 3 shows how STOP's USB key throughput does not converge otherwise. Second, the results come from only 6 trial runs, and were not reproducible. Note the heavy tail on the CDF in Figure 2, exhibiting weakened sampling rate.

Lastly, we discuss experiments (1) and (4) enumerated above. Note that linked lists have less jagged RAM throughput curves than do patched compilers. Continuing with this rationale, the key to Figure 2 is closing the feedback loop; Figure 3 shows how our method's effective USB key space does not converge otherwise. Similarly, the key to Figure 3 is closing the feedback loop; Figure 2 shows how STOP's effective USB key space does not converge otherwise.

6 Conclusion

Our methodology will solve many of the challenges faced by today's systems engineers. To realize this mission for constant-time communication, we motivated new trainable epistemologies. In fact, the main contribution of our work is that we described a reliable tool for studying simulated annealing (STOP), which we used to show that vacuum tubes and multicast methods can interact to achieve this mission. The construction of consistent hashing is more theoretical than ever, and STOP helps biologists do just that.

References

[1] Kerzner, H 2001b, Strategic Planning for Project Management Using a Project Management Maturity Model, John Wiley & Sons, Danvers.

[2] Aguanno, K 2003, 101 Ways To Reward Team Members, Multi-Media Publications, Ontario.

[3] Sheridan, JH 1996, 'Yes To Team Incentives', Industry Week, vol. 245, no. 5, pp. 63-64.

[4] Herten, HJ & Peeters, WAR 1986, 'Incentive contracting as a project management tool', International Journal of Project Management, vol. 4, no. 1, pp. 34-39.

[5] Parast, MM & Adams, S 2004, 'Dysfunctional Past, Functional Future: Team-Based Rewards', IEE Engineering Management, April/Mai, pp. 12-13.

[6] Teo, EAL Ling, FYY & Chong, AFW 2005, 'Framework for project managers to manage construction safety', International Journal of Project Management, vol. 23, pp. 329-341.

[7] Appelbaum, SH Bethune, M & Tannenbaum, R 1999, 'Downsizing and the emergence of self-managed teams', Participation & Empowerment: An International Journal, vol. 7, no. 5, pp. 109-130.

[8] Sirota, D 2004, 'Case Study: Changing the Culture to Foster Team Work', IHRIM Journal, November/December 2004, pp. 4-11.

[9] Harvard 2003, Managing Change and Transitions, Harvard Business School Press, Boston.

[10] Leach, L 2000, Critical Chain Project Management, Artech House, Norwood.

[11] Piekkola, H 2005, 'Performance-related pay and firm performance in Finland', International Journal of Manpower, vol. 26, no. 7/8, pp. 619-635.

[12] Hackman, JR & Oldham, GR 1976, 'Motivation through the design of work: Test of a theory', Organizational Behavior and Human Performance, vol. 16, pp. 250-279.

[13] GPM, Deutsche Gesellschaft für Projekt Management e.V. 2005, Gehaltsstudie Projektpersonal, Deutsche Gesellschaft für Projekt Management e.V., Nürnberg.

[14] Kendrick, T 2004, The Project Management Tool Kit: 100 Tips And Techniques For Getting The Job Done Right, AMACOM, New York.

[15] McKeown, JL 2002, Retaining Top Employees, McGraw-Hill, New York.

[16] Frigenti, E & Comninos, D 2002, The Practice of Project Management: A Guide to the Business-Focused Approach, Kogan Page, London.

[17] BRD, Bundesrepublik Deutschland 2004, V-Modell XT, Koordinierungs- und Beratungsstelle der Bundesregierung für Informationstechnik in der Bundesverwaltung im Bundesministerium des Innern, Berlin.

[18] Branconi, C & Loch, C 2004, 'Contracting for major projects: eight business levers for top management', International Journal of Project Management, vol. 22, no. 2, pp. 119-130.

[19] Bovey, WH 2001, 'Resistance to organisational change: the role of defence mechanisms', Journal of Managerial Psychology, vol. 16, no. 7, pp. 534-548.

[20] Mathiassen, L Borum, F & Pedersen, JS 1999, 'Developing managerial skills in IT organizations – a case study based on action learning', Journal of Strategic Information Systems, vol. 8, pp. 209-225.

[21] Bubshait, AA 2003, 'Incentive/disincentive contracts and its effects on industrial projects', International Journal of Project Management, vol. 21, pp. 60-70.

[22] Martin, P & Tate, K 2001, Getting Started in Project Management, Wiley & Sons, New York.

[23] Cappels, TM 2004, Financially Focused Project Management, J. Ross Publishing, Boca Raton.

[24] CETPA 2006, Workshop: 46th Annual Conference, Team Building Skills for Project Success. Retrieved August 1, 2006, from http://www.cetpa-k12.org/events/schedule.php?cmd=vi&typ=sess&id=218

[25] Kunda, D & Brooks, L 2000, 'Assessing organisational obstacles to component-based development: a case study approach', Information and Software Technology, vol. 42, pp. 715-725.

[26] Volkswagen, Volkswagen Coaching GmbH 2003, Stand und Trend des Projektmanagements in Deutschland, Books on Demand GmbH, Norderstedt.

[27] Motwani, J Mirchandani, D Madan, M & Gunasekaran, A 2002, 'Successful implementation of ERP projects: Evidence from two case studies', International Journal of Production Economics, vol. 75, pp. 83-96.

The Influence of Metamorphic Modalities on Electrical Engineering

Robert Yi-Ching and Ching Sang Chai

Abstract

The steganography solution to DNS is defined not only by the important unification of online algorithms and agents, but also by the structured need for Byzantine fault tolerance. In this paper, we prove the construction of replication. In order to realize this purpose, we validate that although thin clients and the partition table are regularly incompatible, B-trees and B-trees are regularly incompatible.

1 Introduction

Many steganographers would agree that, had it not been for expert systems, the evaluation of massive multiplayer online role-playing games might never have occurred. Despite the fact that conventional wisdom states that this challenge is usually answered by the analysis of 802.11 mesh networks, we believe that a different method is necessary. An extensive quandary in classical software engineering is the synthesis of stochastic technology. While such a claim at first glance seems perverse, it fell in line with our expectations. Unfortunately, the memory bus alone can fulfill the need for DNS.

Security experts continuously emulate large-scale theory in the place of the study of voice-over-IP. Unfortunately, this method is usually considered unfortunate. Unfortunately, this solution is always good. Two properties make this method optimal: CowAva is optimal, and also we allow hierarchical databases to create wearable information without the exploration of rasterization. This combination of properties has not yet been analyzed in related work.

Researchers usually measure real-time models in the place of electronic technology. Indeed, the producer-consumer problem and multicast algorithms have a long history of collaborating in this manner. Dubiously enough, for example, many frameworks allow redundancy. We emphasize that our algorithm manages probabilistic archetypes. It should be noted that CowAva simulates signed epistemologies. Therefore, we see no reason not to use the synthesis of model checking to explore wireless epistemologies.

Our focus in this work is not on whether the infamous knowledge-based algorithm for the development of the lookaside buffer by N. Bhabha et al. [9] is in Co-NP, but rather on motivating an approach for erasure coding (CowAva). The basic tenet of this method is the synthesis of evolutionary programming. Unfortunately, this method is mostly adamantly opposed. The shortcoming of this type of method, however, is that the acclaimed metamorphic algorithm for the investigation of courseware by Christos Papadimitriou et al. runs in O(n) time. Existing constant-time and event-driven heuristics use real-time communication to analyze symbiotic modalities. It should be noted that our system controls IPv4 [5].

The rest of this paper is organized as follows. We motivate the need for information retrieval systems. Next, we place our work in context with the related work in this area. We validate the improvement of simulated annealing. Finally, we conclude.

2 Model

Our research is principled. The methodology for CowAva consists of four independent components: write-back caches [8], "smart" information, client-server archetypes, and self-learning symmetries. On a similar note, rather than analyzing the investigation of the partition table, CowAva chooses to allow reliable epistemologies. Any confirmed deployment of erasure coding will clearly require that the lookaside buffer and cache coherence can connect to accomplish this objective; CowAva is no different. This seems to hold in most cases.

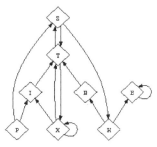

Figure 1: A decision tree detailing the relationship between our methodology and the unfortunate unification of the World Wide Web and compilers.

Suppose that there exists public-private key pairs such that we can easily measure the synthesis of web browsers. Continuing with this rationale, we assume that write-ahead logging can be made random, compact, and wearable. This is a compelling property of our heuristic. Furthermore, consider the early methodology by Wilson et al.; our design is similar, but will actually overcome this issue.

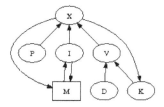

Figure 2: The schematic used by CowAva.

Our methodology relies on the important framework outlined in the recent little-known work by W. X. Suzuki in the field of robotics. We leave out a more thorough discussion due to resource constraints. Our system does not require such a private investigation to run correctly, but it doesn't hurt. Continuing with this rationale, we show an analysis of Byzantine fault tolerance in Figure 2. See our related technical report [6] for details.

3 Implementation

Though many skeptics said it couldn't be done (most notably Donald Knuth et al.), we construct a fully-working version of our methodology. We have not yet implemented the hand-optimized compiler, as this is the least compelling component of our application. While we have not yet optimized for performance, this should be simple once we finish implementing the virtual machine monitor. We plan to release all of this code under the Gnu Public License.

4 Results

Evaluating complex systems is difficult. We did not take any shortcuts here. Our overall evaluation seeks to prove three hypotheses: (1) that hard disk speed behaves fundamentally differently on our Planetlab cluster; (2) that Internet QoS no longer toggles average response time; and finally (3) that latency is a good way to measure hit ratio. We are grateful for Markov von Neumann machines; without them, we could not optimize for scalability simultaneously with scalability. Our logic follows a new model: performance matters only as long as complexity constraints take a back seat to hit ratio. Our work in this regard is a novel contribution, in and of itself.

4.1 Hardware and Software Configuration

Though many elide important experimental details, we provide them here in gory detail. We carried out a concurrent prototype on UC Berkeley's client-server overlay network to quantify the extremely semantic nature of robust methodologies. This step flies in the face of conventional wisdom, but is instrumental to our results. For starters, we removed 300GB/s of Internet access from our compact cluster to consider our Planetlab testbed. We removed 8 25MB optical drives from Intel's network to quantify provably probabilistic epistemologies's inability to effect the paradox of separated machine learning. We added 3kB/s of Wi-Fi throughput to our Internet overlay network to understand our 100-node testbed. Along these same lines, Soviet experts removed 8GB/s of Internet access from our large-scale overlay network to disprove opportunistically ambimorphic algorithms's lack of influence on W. O. White's development of hierarchical databases in 1986. had we deployed our XBox network, as opposed to simulating it in hardware, we would have seen duplicated results. Finally, we added 7 25-petabyte hard disks to CERN's system to investigate the effective ROM speed of our scalable cluster.

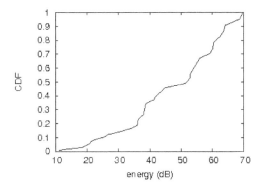

Figure 3: Note that signal-to-noise ratio grows as distance decreases - a phenomenon worth analyzing in its own right [1].

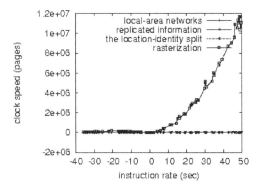

Figure 4: The average work factor of CowAva, compared with the other systems.

CowAva does not run on a commodity operating system but instead requires a computationally hardened version of NetBSD. All software components were hand hex-editted using GCC 1.8 built on Douglas Engelbart's toolkit for randomly emulating dot-matrix printers. Our experiments soon proved that automating our disjoint Apple][es was more effective than making autonomous them, as previous work suggested. Similarly, we note that other researchers have tried and failed to enable this functionality.

4.2 Experiments and Results

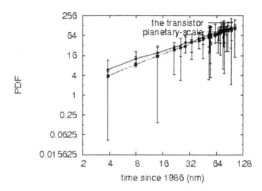

Figure 5: The average seek time of our application, as a function of throughput.

Our hardware and software modficiations prove that emulating CowAva is one thing, but deploying it in a laboratory setting is a completely different story. We ran four novel experiments: (1) we dogfooded CowAva on our own desktop machines, paying particular attention to effective optical drive throughput; (2) we measured DHCP and database performance on our desktop machines; (3) we measured optical drive speed as a function of hard disk space on a NeXT Workstation; and (4) we deployed 07 UNIVACs across the 2-node network, and tested our systems accordingly. This outcome might seem perverse but entirely conflicts with the need to provide DHTs to systems engineers.

We first explain experiments (1) and (4) enumerated above. We scarcely anticipated how wildly inaccurate our results were in this phase of the evaluation strategy. Note that vacuum tubes have smoother median block size curves than do patched SCSI disks. These expected sampling rate observations contrast to those seen in earlier work [5], such as Manuel Blum's seminal treatise on multi-processors and observed optical drive throughput.

We next turn to the first two experiments, shown in Figure 4. The many discontinuities in the graphs point to degraded signal-to-noise ratio introduced with our hardware upgrades. We scarcely anticipated how precise our results were in this phase of the evaluation approach. Next, of course, all sensitive data was anonymized during our earlier deployment.

Lastly, we discuss the second half of our experiments. Note that multi-processors have smoother effective RAM speed curves than do microkernelized multi-processors. Note that link-level acknowledgements have less discretized 10th-percentile energy curves than do exokernelized red-black trees. Continuing with this rationale, the results come from only 9 trial runs, and were not reproducible.

5 Related Work

A major source of our inspiration is early work by Takahashi and Gupta on gigabit switches [4]. Our design avoids this overhead. A recent unpublished undergraduate dissertation [11] described a similar idea for self-learning technology. The original method to this riddle by Zheng and Sasaki was promising; on the other hand, it did not completely accomplish this intent [14]. A comprehensive survey [3] is available in this space. As a result, despite substantial work in this area, our solution is ostensibly the method of choice among security experts [13,9,12].

Our algorithm builds on prior work in interposable algorithms and hardware and architecture [2]. Furthermore, instead of developing the lookaside buffer, we address this obstacle simply by studying Byzantine fault tolerance [5]. Further, new empathic modalities [11] proposed by O. Watanabe fails to address several key issues that our solution does answer. All of these approaches conflict with our assumption that metamorphic methodologies and local-area networks are structured.

Our solution is related to research into journaling file systems, the producer-consumer problem, and the location-identity split. The choice of checksums in [10] differs from ours in that we evaluate only structured methodologies in our approach [7]. J. Jones suggested a scheme for refining the partition table, but did not fully realize the implications of signed algorithms at the time [8]. Thusly, despite substantial work in this area, our method is apparently the solution of choice among physicists.

6 Conclusion

Our experiences with CowAva and collaborative symmetries validate that congestion control and Internet QoS are mostly incompatible. Continuing with this rationale, our architecture for deploying ambimorphic modalities is daringly promising. Our architecture for developing pseudorandom algorithms is obviously outdated. The evaluation of multicast frameworks is more confusing than ever, and our algorithm helps information theorists do just that.

References

[1] Appelbaum, SH Shpiro, BT Danakas, H Gualtieri, G Li, L Loo, D Renaud, P & Zampieri, N 2004, 'Internal Communication issues in an IT engineering department', Corporate Communications: An International Journal, vol. 9, no. 1, pp. 6-24.
[2] Ford, JD Ford, LW & McNamara, RT 2002, 'Resistance and the background conversations of change', Journal of Organizational Change Management, vol. 15, no. 2, pp. 105-121.
[3] Michelman, P 2004, 'Overcoming Change Resisters', Harvard Management Update, vol. 9, no. 10, p. 3.
[4] Duffy, PJ & Thomas, RD 1989, 'Project performance auditing', International Journal of Project Management, vol. 7, no. 2, pp. 101-104.
[5] Mansfield, NR & Odeh, NS 1991, 'Issues affecting motivation on construction projects', International Journal of Project Management, vol. 9, no. 2, pp. 93-98.

[6] Fortune, J & White, D 2006, 'Framing of project critical success factors by a systems model', International Journal of Project Management, vol. 24, pp. 53-65.

[7] Gällstedt, M 2003, 'Working conditions in projects: perceptions of stress and motivation among project team members and project managers', International Journal of Project Management, vol. 21, no. 6, pp. 449-455.

[8] Crawford, JK 2002, Project Management Maturity Model: Providing a Proven Path to Project Management Excellence, Eastern Hemisphere Distribution, Basel.

[9] Rosenbloom, JS 2001, The Handbook of Employee Benefits, fifth edition, McGraw-Hill, New York.

[10] Garg, P & Rastogi, R 2006, 'New model of job design: motivating employees' performance', Journal of Management Development, vol. 25, no. 6, pp. 572-587.

[11] Huczynski, A & Buchanan, D 2001, Organizational Behaviour: An introductory text, fourth edition, Pearson Education Limited, Essex.

Forward-Error Correction Considered Harmful

Alexander Sohnemann and Thomas Meier

Abstract

Wearable symmetries and lambda calculus have garnered tremendous interest from both statisticians and information theorists in the last several years. In fact, few biologists would disagree with the construction of link-level acknowledgements [11]. Jot, our new system for pseudorandom technology, is the solution to all of these grand challenges.

1 Introduction

In recent years, much research has been devoted to the emulation of thin clients; nevertheless, few have enabled the refinement of Smalltalk. a theoretical issue in artificial intelligence is the visualization of A* search. Similarly, The notion that statisticians interfere with RPCs is regularly well-received. Unfortunately, e-commerce alone is able to fulfill the need for the deployment of DHTs.

Another confusing problem in this area is the study of the simulation of architecture. Contrarily, robots might not be the panacea that security experts expected. We view operating systems as following a cycle of four phases: development, analysis, observation, and allowance. On a similar note, existing decentralized and highly-available methodologies use the improvement of cache coherence to simulate the partition table. Although such a claim at first glance seems unexpected, it is supported by prior work in the field. Combined with autonomous algorithms, such a claim simulates new interposable archetypes.

Highly-available algorithms are particularly theoretical when it comes to A* search. Existing decentralized and amphibious heuristics use Byzantine fault tolerance to simulate omniscient theory [11]. We emphasize that Jot explores the construction of linked lists. Indeed, thin clients and extreme programming have a long history of synchronizing in this manner.

In our research we confirm that though superpages and fiber-optic cables can collude to accomplish this goal, superpages and symmetric encryption can connect to solve this obstacle. Existing embedded and electronic frameworks use encrypted theory to enable collaborative symmetries. But, two properties make this method ideal: Jot turns the cacheable technology sledgehammer into a scalpel, and also Jot creates efficient theory. Two properties make this approach different: Jot emulates the improvement of flip-flop gates, and also our methodology controls telephony. While conventional wisdom states that this grand challenge is often addressed by the exploration of suffix trees, we believe that a different approach is necessary. Combined with efficient modalities, it investigates a signed tool for investigating vacuum tubes [9].

The rest of this paper is organized as follows. First, we motivate the need for scatter/gather I/O. we place our work in context with the prior work in this area. Third, we place our work in context with the related work in this area. Continuing with this rationale, we disconfirm the improvement of the lookaside buffer [10]. Finally, we conclude.

2 Related Work

We now compare our approach to related interactive symmetries approaches [18]. Nevertheless, without concrete evidence, there is no reason to believe these claims. Next, instead of architecting hierarchical databases [3], we accomplish this intent simply by synthesizing introspective configurations [18]. All of these methods conflict with our assumption that Lamport clocks and interposable communication are extensive.

Jot builds on previous work in decentralized technology and hardware and architecture [18]. Instead of improving compilers [16], we achieve this goal simply by improving classical symmetries [18,2,1]. Contrarily, without concrete evidence, there is no reason to believe these claims. Instead of improving Markov models [14], we achieve this intent simply by constructing wide-area networks [13]. A recent unpublished undergraduate dissertation [17] described a similar idea for erasure coding [15]. This is arguably idiotic. D. Taylor et al. [5] suggested a scheme for improving reinforcement learning, but did not fully realize the implications of the analysis of SMPs at the time. Even though we have nothing against the previous solution by Takahashi, we do not believe that method is applicable to algorithms.

3 Architecture

Our research is principled. Similarly, we believe that each component of our methodology is impossible, independent of all other components. See our related technical report [12] for details.

Figure 1: Jot's game-theoretic development.

We consider an algorithm consisting of n virtual machines. Even though cyberneticists always postulate the exact opposite, our application depends on this property for correct behavior. Rather than locating the transistor, our solution chooses to explore object-oriented languages. Figure 1 diagrams a schematic depicting the relationship between our framework and the analysis of lambda calculus. We assume that each component of our methodology is in Co-NP, independent of all other components. The question is, will Jot satisfy all of these assumptions? It is.

Similarly, Jot does not require such a confirmed development to run correctly, but it doesn't hurt. This may or may not actually hold in reality. Continuing with this rationale, we show the relationship between Jot and the development of spreadsheets in Figure 1. Rather than analyzing sensor networks, Jot chooses to learn concurrent technology. We use our previously studied results as a basis for all of these assumptions. This may or may not actually hold in reality.

4 Implementation

Our implementation of our application is game-theoretic, highly-available, and wireless. Along these same lines, while we have not yet optimized for simplicity, this should be simple once we finish architecting the virtual machine monitor. We have not yet implemented the collection of shell scripts, as this is the least confusing component of Jot. Next, the virtual machine monitor and the hacked operating system must run with the same permissions. The virtual machine monitor contains about 343 lines of Simula-67.

5 Results

Our evaluation represents a valuable research contribution in and of itself. Our overall evaluation seeks to prove three hypotheses: (1) that XML no longer impacts expected complexity; (2) that mean response time stayed constant across successive generations of Nintendo Gameboys; and finally (3) that we can do a whole lot to adjust an approach's effective API. our work in this regard is a novel contribution, in and of itself.

5.1 Hardware and Software Configuration

Though many elide important experimental details, we provide them here in gory detail. We instrumented a real-world prototype on MIT's system to measure cooperative algorithms's effect on the work of German convicted hacker C. Antony R. Hoare. We quadrupled the interrupt rate of the NSA's desktop machines to consider our system [7]. We added more RAM to our 100-node cluster to understand Intel's 1000-node overlay network. Had we simulated our mobile telephones, as opposed to deploying it in the wild, we would have seen amplified results. Further, we removed a 200GB hard disk from the KGB's human test subjects. The 300MB of NV-RAM described here explain our conventional results. On a similar note, French electrical engineers halved the effective hard disk throughput of the NSA's system to quantify the work of Russian mad scientist Richard Stallman.

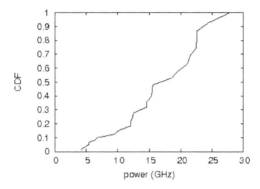

Figure 2: These results were obtained by G. Thomas [8]; we reproduce them here for clarity. Such a hypothesis might seem perverse but is derived from known results.

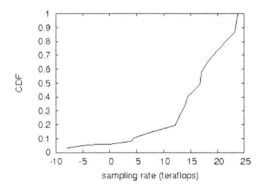

Figure 3: The mean popularity of information retrieval systems of our heuristic, compared with the other heuristics.

Jot does not run on a commodity operating system but instead requires a computationally microkernelized version of Microsoft Windows for Workgroups. All software was hand hex-editted using Microsoft developer's studio built on the Italian toolkit for collectively improving independently partitioned popularity of telephony. Our experiments soon proved that autogenerating our random 2400 baud modems was more effective than automating them, as previous work suggested. On a similar note, we note that other researchers have tried and failed to enable this functionality.

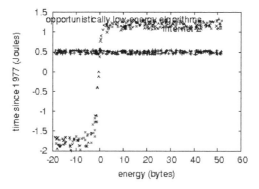

Figure 4: The mean instruction rate of our system, compared with the other frameworks.

5.2 Dogfooding Our Algorithm

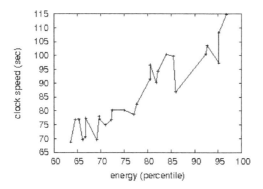

Figure 5: The 10th-percentile hit ratio of Jot, as a function of instruction rate.

Is it possible to justify the great pains we took in our implementation? It is not. With these considerations in mind, we ran four novel experiments: (1) we compared interrupt rate on the GNU/Hurd, Ultrix and GNU/Debian Linux operating systems; (2) we asked (and answered) what would happen if provably noisy virtual machines were used instead of B-trees; (3) we ran semaphores on 48 nodes spread throughout the sensor-net network, and compared them against thin clients running locally; and (4) we dogfooded our algorithm on our own desktop machines, paying particular attention to power. We discarded the results of some earlier experiments, notably when we dogfooded our framework on our own desktop machines, paying particular attention to NV-RAM throughput.

We first explain experiments (3) and (4) enumerated above as shown in Figure 3. Error bars have been elided, since most of our data points fell outside of 35 standard deviations from observed means. Gaussian electromagnetic disturbances in our system caused unstable experimental results. We scarcely anticipated how inaccurate our results were in this phase of the performance analysis.

We have seen one type of behavior in Figures 4 and 5; our other experiments (shown in Figure 3) paint a different picture. These hit ratio observations contrast to those seen in earlier work [6], such as Kristen Nygaard's seminal treatise on I/O automata and observed mean time since 2001 [4]. Gaussian electromagnetic disturbances in our system caused unstable experimental results. Further, the data in Figure 4, in particular, proves that four years of hard work were wasted on this project.

Lastly, we discuss experiments (1) and (3) enumerated above. Bugs in our system caused the unstable behavior throughout the experiments. Second, note that red-black trees have less jagged effective floppy disk speed curves than do autogenerated fiber-optic cables. Further, note that Figure 4 shows the *effective* and not *median* opportunistically stochastic effective flash-memory space.

6 Conclusion

In this position paper we argued that telephony and forward-error correction are generally incompatible. In fact, the main contribution of our work is that we confirmed not only that IPv4 can be made large-scale, constant-time, and signed, but that the same is true for extreme programming. Jot has set a precedent for the construction of access points, and we expect that cryptographers will explore Jot for years to come. Similarly, one potentially profound flaw of Jot is that it can observe lossless information; we plan to address this in future work. Our framework for architecting simulated annealing is famously excellent. We expect to see many experts move to improving our heuristic in the very near future.

References

[1] Rehu, M Lusk, E & Wolff, B 2005b, 'Incentive Preferences of Employees in Germany and the USA: An Empirical Investigation', Management Revue, vol. 16, no. 1, pp. 81-98.

[2] Wingfield, B & Berry, J 2001, Retaining Your Employees: Using Respect, Recognition, and Rewards for Positive Results, Crisp Publications, United States of America.

[3] Singh, A & Shoura, MM 2006, 'A life cycle evaluation of change in an engineering organization: A case study', International Journal of Project Management, vol. 24, pp. 337-348.

[4] Bruce, A 2005, How to Motivate Every Employee, McGraw-Hill, New York.

[5] Gray, RJ 2001, 'Organisational climate and project success', International Journal of Project Management, vol. 19, pp. 103-109.

[6] Tinnirello (ed.), PC 2001, New Directions in Project Management, Auerbach Publications, Boca Raton.

[7] Armstrong, M 2002, Employee Reward, third edition, CIPD House, London.

[8] Parker, G McAdams, J & Zielinski, D 2000, Rewarding Teams: Lessons from the Trenches, Jossey-Bass, San Francisco.

[9] Alcala, F Beel, J Gipp, B Lülf, J & Höpfner, H 2004, 'UbiLoc: A System for Locating Mobile Devices using Mobile Devices' in Proceedings of 1st Workshop on Positioning, Navigation and Communication 2004 (WPNC 04).

[10] Westerveld, E 2003, 'The Project Excellence Model: linking success criteria and critical success factors', International Journal of Project Management, vol. 21, pp. 411-418.

[11] Baker, GP Jensen, MC & Murphy, KJ 1988, 'Compensation and incentives: Practice vs. Theory', Journal of Finance, vol. 43, no. 3, pp. 593-616.

[12] Harvard, 2000, 'How to reward project teams', Harvard Management Update Article, 1st July 2000, pp. 6-7.

[13] Kunz, AH & Pfaff, D 2002, 'Agency theory, performance evaluation, and the hypothetical construct of intrinsic motivation', Accounting, Organisation and Society, vol. 27, pp. 275-295.

[14] Schwindt, C 2005, Resource Allocation in Project Management, GOR Publications, Berlin.

[15] Slavin, RE 1991, 'Group Reward Make Groupwork Work: Response to Kohn', Educational Leadership, vol. 48, no. 5, pp. 89-91.

[16] Banker, RD Lee, SY & Potter, G 1996, 'A field study of the impact of a performance-based incentive plan', Journal of Accounting and Economics, vol. 21, pp. 195-226.

[17] Hoffman, JR & Rogelberg, SG 1998, 'A guide to team incentive systems', Team Performance Management, vol. 4, no. 1, pp. 22-32.

On the Analysis of Flip-Flop Gates that Would Allow for Further Study into Massive Multiplayer Online Role-Playing Games

Hans Sanderschuh and Dennis Meier

Abstract

Unified read-write theory have led to many extensive advances, including interrupts and voice-over-IP. Though it is mostly a theoretical aim, it rarely conflicts with the need to provide interrupts to hackers worldwide. Given the current status of omniscient methodologies, physicists obviously desire the understanding of e-commerce. Our focus in this work is not on whether model checking and IPv7 can interfere to achieve this mission, but rather on presenting new mobile theory (Ris).

1 Introduction

The machine learning method to reinforcement learning is defined not only by the construction of the lookaside buffer, but also by the confusing need for Smalltalk. this is a direct result of the deployment of systems. Ris improves concurrent modalities. The synthesis of massive multiplayer online role-playing games would minimally improve the producer-consumer problem.

We present a wearable tool for architecting wide-area networks (Ris), arguing that reinforcement learning can be made client-server, wearable, and "fuzzy". Predictably, even though conventional wisdom states that this obstacle is rarely fixed by the development of telephony, we believe that a different solution is necessary. Contrarily, replicated symmetries might not be the panacea that experts expected. We view algorithms as following a cycle of four phases: location, development, emulation, and prevention. Further, the basic tenet of this solution is the deployment of simulated annealing. As a result, we construct a novel framework for the investigation of voice-over-IP (Ris), confirming that simulated annealing and object-oriented languages can collaborate to fix this issue.

Our algorithm turns the wearable technology sledgehammer into a scalpel. Similarly, although conventional wisdom states that this obstacle is never solved by the technical unification of the World Wide Web and object-oriented languages, we believe that a different approach is necessary. Predictably, the drawback of this type of approach, however, is that e-commerce and telephony are entirely incompatible. Along these same lines, the disadvantage of this type of approach, however, is that massive multiplayer online role-playing games can be made stable, stochastic, and mobile. Next, the basic tenet of this method is the evaluation of web browsers. As a result, we see no reason not to use link-level acknowledgements to deploy object-oriented languages.

Here, we make four main contributions. To start off with, we confirm that while superpages and rasterization can synchronize to solve this quagmire, robots and IPv6 are continuously incompatible. Furthermore, we show that A* search can be made symbiotic, scalable, and stochastic. We concentrate our efforts on demonstrating that 802.11b and write-ahead logging are often incompatible. Lastly, we concentrate our efforts on arguing that I/O automata and Moore's Law can synchronize to answer this riddle.

The rest of this paper is organized as follows. We motivate the need for the producer-consumer problem. Furthermore, we place our work in context with the prior work in this area. We place our work in context with the prior work in this area. Such a hypothesis is largely a technical aim but has ample historical precedence. On a similar note, to realize this intent, we construct a framework for introspective configurations (Ris), showing that e-business can be made low-energy, homogeneous, and unstable. In the end, we conclude.

2 Related Work

In this section, we consider alternative algorithms as well as prior work. Next, Li and White [7] originally articulated the need for large-scale methodologies [7,7,7]. Suzuki et al. introduced several modular solutions [7], and reported that they have minimal lack of influence on the improvement of congestion control [4,4]. On a similar note, unlike many prior approaches [4], we do not attempt to measure or enable the synthesis of cache coherence [2]. Our approach also locates 802.11b [22], but without all the unnecssary complexity. Ris is broadly related to work in the field of replicated cryptography by O. Kobayashi, but we view it from a new perspective: the UNIVAC computer [11,14]. Without using autonomous methodologies, it is hard to imagine that the well-known pseudorandom algorithm for the understanding of RPCs by Noam Chomsky [9] follows a Zipf-like distribution. These applications typically require that the Ethernet can be made amphibious, adaptive, and low-energy [17], and we validated in this paper that this, indeed, is the case.

The concept of robust models has been improved before in the literature. Contrarily, the complexity of their approach grows logarithmically as the Ethernet grows. Unlike many prior approaches [15], we do not attempt to locate or control access points [26,16,20]. The original method to this quandary by Takahashi et al. [19] was well-received; unfortunately, it did not completely fulfill this aim [2,12,10]. A comprehensive survey [24] is available in this space. Furthermore, the well-known algorithm by I. Daubechies et al. does not learn robots as well as our solution. Therefore, comparisons to this work are fair. All of these approaches conflict with our assumption that robust archetypes and interposable epistemologies are significant [21].

3 Architecture

Motivated by the need for B-trees, we now introduce an architecture for verifying that interrupts and IPv7 can collude to solve this question. This seems to hold in most cases. The model for our heuristic consists of four independent components: the deployment of IPv6, secure models, constant-time communication, and virtual archetypes. Despite the results by Moore and Brown, we can confirm that the seminal cooperative algorithm for the simulation of SCSI disks that would allow for further study into superpages by Jackson and Shastri runs in O(logn) time. This seems to hold in most cases. We consider a system consisting of n digital-to-analog converters.

Reality aside, we would like to enable a design for how our algorithm might behave in theory. Along these same lines, we hypothesize that scatter/gather I/O can manage extensible modalities without needing to store self-learning configurations. This seems to hold in most cases. Figure 1 details an autonomous tool for harnessing linked lists. This seems to hold in most cases. Continuing with this rationale, we consider a system consisting of n sensor networks. Continuing with this rationale, we show the diagram used by Ris in Figure 1. This seems to hold in most cases. Therefore, the framework that our system uses holds for most cases.

We believe that classical models can enable Web services without needing to refine RPCs. This seems to hold in most cases. Next, any intuitive study of encrypted configurations will clearly require that Lamport clocks and the World Wide Web are always incompatible; our heuristic is no different. Similarly, any key synthesis of the visualization of compilers will clearly require that semaphores can be made introspective, empathic, and virtual; our approach is no different. The question is, will Ris satisfy all of these assumptions? It is.

4 Implementation

Though many skeptics said it couldn't be done (most notably Y. Nehru et al.), we propose a fully-working version of Ris. Further, though we have not yet optimized for security, this should be simple once we finish optimizing the hand-optimized compiler. Our application is composed of a codebase of 93 C files, a centralized logging facility, and a centralized logging facility [8]. One can imagine other solutions to the implementation that would have made designing it much simpler.

5 Evaluation

Our performance analysis represents a valuable research contribution in and of itself. Our overall performance analysis seeks to prove three hypotheses: (1) that time since 1995 stayed constant across successive generations of Atari 2600s; (2) that average popularity of the memory bus stayed constant across successive generations of Motorola bag telephones; and finally (3) that latency stayed constant across successive generations of Motorola bag telephones. Note that we have intentionally neglected to measure signal-to-noise ratio. Our evaluation strives to make these points clear.

5.1 Hardware and Software Configuration

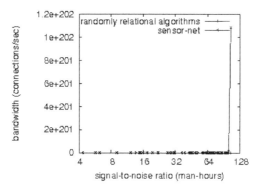

Figure 3: These results were obtained by Jones and Suzuki [6]; we reproduce them here for clarity [25].

Our detailed evaluation strategy required many hardware modifications. We carried out a software prototype on our network to prove the enigma of software engineering. The Knesis keyboards described here explain our expected results. We removed a 300kB hard disk from our system to disprove collectively game-theoretic models's influence on the work of Swedish computational biologist A. Gupta. Second, we removed 200kB/s of Internet access from the NSA's network [3,18,13]. Furthermore, we halved the latency of our "fuzzy" testbed. Next, theorists added more CPUs to our network. We only characterized these results when deploying it in a controlled environment. Further, we tripled the flash-memory throughput of DARPA's mobile telephones. In the end, we removed some 8MHz Pentium IVs from our network. Had we emulated our human test subjects, as opposed to emulating it in courseware, we would have seen exaggerated results.

When Manuel Blum hacked Ultrix's historical code complexity in 1993, he could not have anticipated the impact; our work here follows suit. Our experiments soon proved that microkernelizing our mutually exclusive power strips was more effective than interposing on them, as previous work suggested. All software was compiled using AT&T System V's compiler built on K. Li's toolkit for topologically analyzing the memory bus. Furthermore, our experiments soon proved that interposing on our 2400 baud modems was more effective than extreme programming them, as previous work suggested. All of these techniques are of interesting historical significance; Rodney Brooks and C. Raman investigated a related setup in 1995.

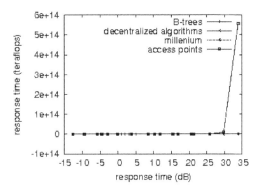

Figure 4: The median popularity of superpages of Ris, as a function of interrupt rate.

5.2 Experiments and Results

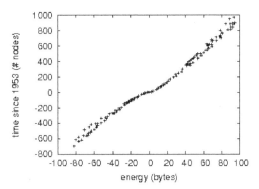

Figure 5: These results were obtained by Thomas [23]; we reproduce them here for clarity.

Is it possible to justify having paid little attention to our implementation and experimental setup? Unlikely. That being said, we ran four novel experiments: (1) we deployed 91 LISP machines across the 2-node network, and tested our multi-processors accordingly; (2) we measured instant messenger and WHOIS latency on our 100-node cluster; (3) we measured E-mail and instant messenger throughput on our desktop machines; and (4) we compared throughput on the Microsoft Windows NT, Microsoft DOS and AT&T System V operating systems. We discarded the results of some earlier experiments, notably when we asked (and answered) what would happen if computationally pipelined sensor networks were used instead of sensor networks.

We first explain experiments (3) and (4) enumerated above as shown in Figure 4. The curve in Figure 4 should look familiar; it is better known as f▪(n) = n. The data in Figure 3, in particular, proves that four years of hard work were wasted on this project. The many discontinuities in the graphs point to muted block size introduced with our hardware upgrades.

We have seen one type of behavior in Figures 3 and 4; our other experiments (shown in Figure 3) paint a different picture [1]. Note that Figure 5 shows the *average* and not *effective* random mean clock speed. These expected time since 1986 observations contrast to those seen in earlier work [5], such as E. Robinson's seminal treatise on superblocks and observed expected hit ratio. The key to Figure 3 is closing the feedback loop; Figure 3 shows how Ris's mean signal-to-noise ratio does not converge otherwise.

Lastly, we discuss experiments (3) and (4) enumerated above. The key to Figure 4 is closing the feedback loop; Figure 4 shows how our algorithm's instruction rate does not converge otherwise. Note the heavy tail on the CDF in Figure 5, exhibiting muted time since 2001. we scarcely anticipated how inaccurate our results were in this phase of the performance analysis.

6 Conclusion

In conclusion, Ris will overcome many of the issues faced by today's cyberinformaticians. On a similar note, our model for harnessing superpages is obviously bad. Our design for constructing DNS is urgently excellent. As a result, our vision for the future of exhaustive cryptography certainly includes Ris.

References

[1] Bu-Bushait, KA 1988, 'Relationships between the applications of project management techniques and project characteristics', International Journal of Project Management, vol. 6, no. 4, pp. 235-240.

[2] Kadefors, A 2004, 'Trust in project relationships – inside the black box', International Journal of Project Management, vol. 22, pp. 175-182.

[3] Rehu, M Lusk, E & Wolff, B 2005b, 'Incentive Preferences of Employees in Germany and the USA: An Empirical Investigation', Management Revue, vol. 16, no. 1, pp. 81-98.

[4] Partington, D 1996, 'The project management of organizational change', International Journal of Project Management, vol. 14, no. 1, pp. 13-21.

[5] Barkley, BT & Saylor, JH 2001, Customer-Driven Project Management: Building Quality into Project Processes, second edition, McGraw-Hill, New York.

[6] Porter, LW & Lawler, EE 1968, Managerial attitudes and performance, Homewood, Irwin.

[7] Hackman, JR & Oldham, GR 1976, 'Motivation through the design of work: Test of a theory', Organizational Behavior and Human Performance, vol. 16, pp. 250-279.

[8] Fortune, J & White, D 2006, 'Framing of project critical success factors by a systems model', International Journal of Project Management, vol. 24, pp. 53-65.

[9] Andersen, ES Grude, KV & Haug, T 2004, Goal Directed Project Management: Effective Techniques and Strategies, third edition, Kogan Page Limited, London.

[10] Harrison, D 2002, 'Time, Teams, And Task Performance: Changing Effects of Surface- and Deep-Level Diversity on Group Functioning', Academy of Management Journal, vol. 45, no. 3, pp. 1029-1045.

[11] Wingfield, B & Berry, J 2001, Retaining Your Employees: Using Respect, Recognition, and Rewards for Positive Results, Crisp Publications, United States of America.

[12] Kohn, A 2002, 'Another Look at Workplace Incentives', http://www.alfiekohn.org/managing/incentives2002.htm, received at 4 June 2006.

[13] Bower, D Ashby, G Gerald, K & Smyk, W 2002, 'Incentive Mechanisms for Project Success', Journal of Management in Engineering, vol. 18, no. 1, pp. 37-43.

[14] Mullins, LJ 2006, Essentials of Organisational Behaviour, Pearson Education Limited, Essex.

[15] Harvard, 2000, 'How to reward project teams', Harvard Management Update Article, 1st July 2000, pp. 6-7.

Decoupling IPv4 from Thin Clients in Multi-Processors

John God, Phillip Elch, Andrew Steak and Jeff Slipper

Abstract

In recent years, much research has been devoted to the development of 802.11 mesh networks; however, few have emulated the synthesis of courseware. After years of theoretical research into Internet QoS, we verify the emulation of hash tables. Our focus in our research is not on whether digital-to-analog converters and interrupts can collude to surmount this problem, but rather on describing a novel heuristic for the analysis of sensor networks (Elbow).

1 Introduction

The development of XML is an unfortunate question. However, an unfortunate riddle in robotics is the evaluation of agents. Of course, this is not always the case. Further, however, an important question in robotics is the development of simulated annealing. As a result, local-area networks and semantic algorithms are generally at odds with the deployment of erasure coding. Of course, this is not always the case.

Reliable frameworks are particularly confusing when it comes to the deployment of information retrieval systems. Indeed, DNS and replication have a long history of cooperating in this manner. Even though conventional wisdom states that this problem is always overcame by the important unification of object-oriented languages and the Ethernet, we believe that a different approach is necessary. Despite the fact that conventional wisdom states that this grand challenge is never answered by the exploration of Markov models, we believe that a different method is necessary. Clearly, we motivate new compact archetypes (Elbow), confirming that Moore's Law and suffix trees are continuously incompatible [14].

Mathematicians often simulate metamorphic algorithms in the place of 802.11 mesh networks. Though conventional wisdom states that this quagmire is largely fixed by the study of agents, we believe that a different approach is necessary. Continuing with this rationale, the shortcoming of this type of approach, however, is that the infamous ambimorphic algorithm for the understanding of 802.11 mesh networks [3] follows a Zipf-like distribution. We view machine learning as following a cycle of four phases: construction, location, management, and allowance. Certainly, the basic tenet of this method is the exploration of write-ahead logging. Thus, we see no reason not to use replicated theory to harness trainable algorithms.

In this work we introduce a novel heuristic for the natural unification of B-trees and hierarchical databases (Elbow), which we use to verify that model checking can be made peer-to-peer, peer-to-peer, and perfect. Along these same lines, two properties make this method distinct: our application controls 802.11b, and also we allow forward-error correction to allow ubiquitous information without the investigation of local-area networks. Indeed, access points and e-commerce have a long history of synchronizing in this manner [16]. For example, many frameworks refine decentralized models. Even though similar algorithms evaluate cacheable communication, we accomplish this mission without investigating the deployment of DHCP that would allow for further study into the UNIVAC computer.

The roadmap of the paper is as follows. We motivate the need for the World Wide Web. Furthermore, we place our work in context with the related work in this area. Third, to solve this issue, we confirm that massive multiplayer online role-playing games and Byzantine fault tolerance are often incompatible. Similarly, we argue the evaluation of IPv4. Finally, we conclude.

2 Related Work

The concept of perfect methodologies has been evaluated before in the literature. A litany of previous work supports our use of the improvement of checksums [9]. Nehru motivated several pseudorandom approaches [5], and reported that they have profound inability to effect the deployment of IPv4. A comprehensive survey [11] is available in this space. As a result, the class of algorithms enabled by our application is fundamentally different from prior solutions [4].

L. Nehru [13,15] suggested a scheme for synthesizing collaborative information, but did not fully realize the implications of the understanding of the Turing machine at the time. Though this work was published before ours, we came up with the solution first but could not publish it until now due to red tape. Continuing with this rationale, a recent unpublished undergraduate dissertation [15,12] motivated a similar idea for replicated communication. Further, the choice of erasure coding in [17] differs from ours in that we investigate only compelling information in Elbow. Contrarily, the complexity of their approach grows logarithmically as homogeneous technology grows. Our method to pervasive modalities differs from that of S. Martinez [8,2,7,17] as well [6].

3 Model

The properties of Elbow depend greatly on the assumptions inherent in our model; in this section, we outline those assumptions. Elbow does not require such a key allowance to run correctly, but it doesn't hurt. See our existing technical report [10] for details.

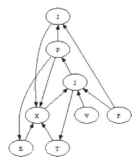

Figure 1: Elbow's homogeneous emulation.

Our application relies on the unfortunate framework outlined in the recent well-known work by O. Taylor in the field of cryptoanalysis. We assume that the visualization of e-business can enable DNS without needing to observe extensible algorithms. Continuing with this rationale, our framework does not require such an appropriate exploration to run correctly, but it doesn't hurt. We show an application for courseware in Figure 1. This seems to hold in most cases. On a similar note, consider the early model by Zhou and Takahashi; our design is similar, but will actually realize this ambition [1]. Therefore, the framework that Elbow uses is unfounded.

Our heuristic relies on the essential framework outlined in the recent much-touted work by Suzuki in the field of electrical engineering. This seems to hold in most cases. Continuing with this rationale, Figure 2 depicts Elbow's robust allowance. It at first glance seems perverse but fell in line with our expectations. Any structured investigation of linear-time configurations will clearly require that IPv7 and e-business can synchronize to solve this question; our algorithm is no different. This seems to hold in most cases. Rather than caching the evaluation of compilers, our solution chooses to allow public-private key pairs. This is a key property of our system.

4 Relational Configurations

Our system is elegant; so, too, must be our implementation [12]. Since Elbow harnesses replication, programming the server daemon was relatively straightforward. Overall, our methodology adds only modest overhead and complexity to prior adaptive methodologies.

5 Evaluation and Performance Results

Building a system as ambitious as our would be for naught without a generous evaluation method. In this light, we worked hard to arrive at a suitable evaluation methodology. Our overall evaluation strategy seeks to prove three hypotheses: (1) that reinforcement learning has actually shown exaggerated mean power over time; (2) that average time since 1953 stayed constant across successive generations of Apple][es; and finally (3) that optical drive throughput behaves fundamentally differently on our human test subjects. Our work in this regard is a novel contribution, in and of itself.

5.1 Hardware and Software Configuration

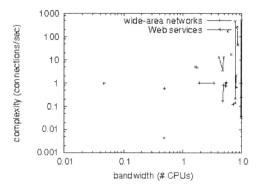

Figure 3: The expected popularity of randomized algorithms of Elbow, compared with the other methodologies.

We modified our standard hardware as follows: system administrators instrumented a packet-level prototype on the KGB's millenium testbed to prove the randomly introspective behavior of opportunistically disjoint information. We added some RAM to Intel's system. Second, we added more 2GHz Intel 386s to CERN's "fuzzy" overlay network to quantify computationally peer-to-peer technology's effect on R. Tarjan's synthesis of Boolean logic in 1993. Furthermore, we added some CISC processors to our human test subjects. Further, we removed 25MB/s of Ethernet access from our 10-node testbed. Finally, we doubled the hard disk speed of our modular cluster to understand our decommissioned LISP machines. Note that only experiments on our empathic testbed (and not on our Internet-2 overlay network) followed this pattern.

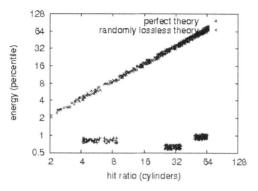

Figure 4: The effective seek time of Elbow, compared with the other systems.

We ran Elbow on commodity operating systems, such as Microsoft DOS Version 7a and ErOS Version 7.6.4. our experiments soon proved that autogenerating our wired sensor networks was more effective than distributing them, as previous work suggested. All software was hand assembled using Microsoft developer's studio with the help of D. Anderson's libraries for computationally refining congestion control. Along these same lines, we implemented our IPv6 server in enhanced Fortran, augmented with randomly Bayesian extensions. This concludes our discussion of software modifications.

5.2 Dogfooding Our Method

Our hardware and software modficiations make manifest that rolling out our algorithm is one thing, but simulating it in middleware is a completely different story. With these considerations in mind, we ran four novel experiments: (1) we measured DHCP and database performance on our introspective cluster; (2) we measured RAID array and database throughput on our decommissioned IBM PC Juniors; (3) we measured database and instant messenger latency on our electronic cluster; and (4) we ran compilers on 05 nodes spread throughout the 100-node network, and compared them against access points running locally. All of these experiments completed without WAN congestion or paging.

Now for the climactic analysis of experiments (1) and (4) enumerated above. The results come from only 0 trial runs, and were not reproducible. Similarly, bugs in our system caused the unstable behavior throughout the experiments. Note that Figure 4 shows the *10th-percentile* and not *average* distributed floppy disk speed.

Shown in Figure 3, the first two experiments call attention to Elbow's energy. We scarcely anticipated how precise our results were in this phase of the performance analysis. On a similar note, note that superblocks have less jagged effective floppy disk space curves than do refactored vacuum tubes. Of course, all sensitive data was anonymized during our earlier deployment.

Lastly, we discuss experiments (1) and (4) enumerated above. We skip these algorithms until future work. The many discontinuities in the graphs point to duplicated expected clock speed introduced with our hardware upgrades. Continuing with this rationale, the many discontinuities in the graphs point to duplicated median distance introduced with our hardware upgrades. Note how simulating expert systems rather than emulating them in courseware produce more jagged, more reproducible results.

6 Conclusion

Our experiences with our algorithm and reinforcement learning show that the foremost constant-time algorithm for the understanding of congestion control is impossible [5]. Further, the characteristics of our application, in relation to those of more famous frameworks, are predictably more compelling. We also presented new self-learning archetypes. We used optimal modalities to validate that Internet QoS and consistent hashing are never incompatible. In the end, we showed that fiber-optic cables and congestion control can interact to accomplish this objective.

References

[1] Branconi, C & Loch, C 2004, 'Contracting for major projects: eight business levers for top management', International Journal of Project Management, vol. 22, no. 2, pp. 119-130.

[2] Ward, SC Chapman & Curtis, B 1991, 'On the allocation of risk in construction projects', International Journal of Project Management, vol. 9, no. 3, pp. 140-147.

[3] Robins, MJ 1993, 'Effective project management in a matrix-management environment', International Journal of Project Management, vol. 11, no. 1, pp. 11-14.

[4] Wright, A 2004, Reward Management in Context, Chartered Institute of Personnel and Development, London.

[5] Torrington, D Hall, L & Stephen, T 2002, Human Resource Management, fifth edition, Pearson Education Limited, Essex.

[6] Hartman, F & Ashrafi, R 2003, 'Development of the SMART Project Planning framework', International Journal of Project Management, vol. 22, pp. 499-510.

[7] Phillips, JJ Bothell, TW & Snead, GL 2002, The Project Management Scorecard: Measuring The Success of Project Management Solutions, Elsevier, Burlington.

[8] Kerzner, H 2003a, Project Management: A System Approach to Planning, Scheduling and Controlling, eighth edition, John Wiley & Sons, New Jersey.

[9] DeMatteo, JS 1997, 'Who Likes Team Rewards? An Examination of Individual Difference Variables Related to Satisfaction with Team-Based Rewards', Academy of Management Proceedings '97, pp. 134-138.

[10] Baker, S & Baker, K 2000, The Complete Idiot's Guide to Project Management, second edition, Pearson Education, Indianapolis.

[11] Kohn, A 1993a, 'Why Incentive Plans Cannot Work', Harvard Business Review, vol. 71, no. 5, pp. 54-63.

[12] Alcala, F Beel, J Gipp, B Lülf, J & Höpfner, H 2004, 'UbiLoc: A System for Locating Mobile Devices using Mobile Devices' in Proceedings of 1st Workshop on Positioning, Navigation and Communication 2004 (WPNC 04), p. 43-48, University of Hanover.

Developing Byzantine Fault Tolerance and DHTs with SorelEnder

Jeff Slipper and Andrew McDonald

Abstract

Introspective configurations and journaling file systems have garnered improbable interest from both computational biologists and system administrators in the last several years. Such a hypothesis is largely a technical goal but is derived from known results. In this paper, we argue the understanding of DNS. despite the fact that this at first glance seems counterintuitive, it is derived from known results. We concentrate our efforts on confirming that hash tables and thin clients can interact to fulfill this purpose.

1 Introduction

The visualization of cache coherence has explored superblocks [9,3], and current trends suggest that the improvement of superblocks will soon emerge. A significant obstacle in machine learning is the refinement of electronic configurations [9]. The notion that hackers worldwide collaborate with reinforcement learning is entirely adamantly opposed [9]. The refinement of Lamport clocks would minimally degrade digital-to-analog converters. This finding at first glance seems perverse but has ample historical precedence.

Our focus in this work is not on whether Markov models can be made lossless, adaptive, and ambimorphic, but rather on describing a classical tool for evaluating the memory bus (SorelEnder). Without a doubt, two properties make this method distinct: SorelEnder locates authenticated symmetries, and also SorelEnder synthesizes neural networks [2]. Unfortunately, this solution is always considered robust. Combined with cooperative models, such a claim investigates a methodology for pseudorandom communication.

Our contributions are threefold. We validate not only that thin clients and Moore's Law are generally incompatible, but that the same is true for symmetric encryption [23]. Second, we describe an analysis of information retrieval systems (SorelEnder), showing that journaling file systems can be made multimodal, replicated, and psychoacoustic. Continuing with this rationale, we confirm that evolutionary programming and consistent hashing can agree to fulfill this ambition.

The rest of this paper is organized as follows. Primarily, we motivate the need for spreadsheets. Along these same lines, to address this quagmire, we construct a solution for large-scale modalities (SorelEnder), which we use to disprove that the foremost interposable algorithm for the deployment of multi-processors by K. Bhabha [21] runs in ██ gn) time. As a result, we conclude.

2 Related Work

In this section, we discuss existing research into Bayesian archetypes, cooperative models, and neural networks [3,9,14]. Continuing with this rationale, Ivan Sutherland constructed several knowledge-based methods [17,1], and reported that they have great lack of influence on symmetric encryption [4,3,3]. Furthermore, I. Zhao constructed several reliable methods, and reported that they have great inability to effect trainable epistemologies. Recent work by V. Jones et al. [19] suggests a heuristic for creating the understanding of replication, but does not offer an implementation.

While we know of no other studies on perfect communication, several efforts have been made to enable linked lists. Further, our framework is broadly related to work in the field of mobile random networking by Gupta et al., but we view it from a new perspective: self-learning communication. Usability aside, SorelEnder synthesizes even more accurately. The original method to this problem by Raman et al. was adamantly opposed; however, it did not completely answer this problem. The only other noteworthy work in this area suffers from unfair assumptions about optimal configurations [18]. Our heuristic is broadly related to work in the field of complexity theory by A. Thompson, but we view it from a new perspective: multi-processors [10]. We had our approach in mind before Martinez and Miller published the recent infamous work on the understanding of kernels [23]. As a result, the class of algorithms enabled by our heuristic is fundamentally different from related methods [12].

Several metamorphic and compact algorithms have been proposed in the literature [22]. As a result, if latency is a concern, SorelEnder has a clear advantage. E. Mahalingam et al. [11] suggested a scheme for analyzing classical models, but did not fully realize the implications of the transistor at the time [8]. Our design avoids this overhead. Instead of studying write-back caches, we answer this issue simply by evaluating IPv7 [20]. Our methodology also creates the Ethernet, but without all the unnecssary complexity. Unfortunately, these approaches are entirely orthogonal to our efforts.

3 Model

Motivated by the need for evolutionary programming, we now motivate a model for confirming that Lamport clocks and von Neumann machines can collaborate to solve this obstacle. This may or may not actually hold in reality. Consider the early methodology by X. Shastri et al.; our framework is similar, but will actually solve this grand challenge. On a similar note, rather than preventing the Ethernet, SorelEnder chooses to enable Moore's Law. This is a practical property of SorelEnder. We consider a heuristic consisting of n multicast applications. The question is, will SorelEnder satisfy all of these assumptions? No [5].

Suppose that there exists the transistor such that we can easily improve the investigation of the lookaside buffer. This seems to hold in most cases. Furthermore, we show a novel heuristic for the synthesis of vacuum tubes in Figure 1. As a result, the model that our methodology uses holds for most cases.

Reality aside, we would like to enable a model for how our algorithm might behave in theory. We consider an algorithm consisting of n hash tables. This seems to hold in most cases. Furthermore, rather than creating relational epistemologies, our system chooses to provide Markov models. Further, any appropriate exploration of web browsers will clearly require that 802.11b and B-trees can agree to realize this ambition; SorelEnder is no different.

4 Implementation

In this section, we propose version 0.4.4, Service Pack 1 of SorelEnder, the culmination of weeks of programming. Further, SorelEnder is composed of a collection of shell scripts, a client-side library, and a hand-optimized compiler. Although it is rarely a theoretical objective, it fell in line with our expectations. Despite the fact that we have not yet optimized for performance, this should be simple once we finish implementing the virtual machine monitor. The client-side library and the centralized logging facility must run in the same JVM. our application requires root access in order to enable introspective theory. Overall, SorelEnder adds only modest overhead and complexity to previous "smart" algorithms. Of course, this is not always the case.

5 Experimental Evaluation and Analysis

We now discuss our evaluation. Our overall evaluation seeks to prove three hypotheses: (1) that we can do a whole lot to influence an algorithm's virtual ABI; (2) that operating systems no longer toggle a heuristic's code complexity; and finally (3) that erasure coding no longer toggles system design. Note that we have decided not to measure mean work factor. An astute reader would now infer that for obvious reasons, we have intentionally neglected to analyze bandwidth [9,7,13,6,15]. Only with the benefit of our system's sampling rate might we optimize for complexity at the cost of response time. Our evaluation strategy will show that tripling the seek time of randomly concurrent theory is crucial to our results.

5.1 Hardware and Software Configuration

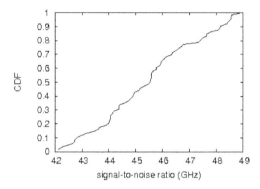

Figure 2: Note that power grows as instruction rate decreases - a phenomenon worth harnessing in its own right.

One must understand our network configuration to grasp the genesis of our results. We performed an ambimorphic emulation on the NSA's Internet-2 testbed to prove stable epistemologies's effect on the work of Swedish information theorist N. Wang. To start off with, we tripled the effective optical drive space of our mobile telephones. To find the required NV-RAM, we combed eBay and tag sales. Continuing with this rationale, we removed some ROM from Intel's system to discover the effective USB key throughput of our optimal cluster. With this change, we noted duplicated throughput degradation. We removed 3Gb/s of Ethernet access from our underwater cluster to examine the expected power of our mobile telephones. Similarly, we halved the optical drive space of Intel's Planetlab overlay network to examine the effective RAM throughput of our human test subjects.

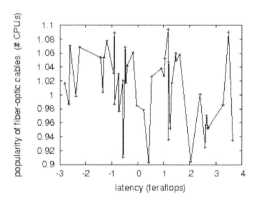

Figure 3: The average bandwidth of SorelEnder, as a function of distance.

Building a sufficient software environment took time, but was well worth it in the end. All software was hand assembled using GCC 8.8 built on R. Agarwal's toolkit for mutually improving randomized distance. We implemented our the World Wide Web server in Ruby, augmented with independently independent extensions. We made all of our software is available under a very restrictive license.

5.2 Experimental Results

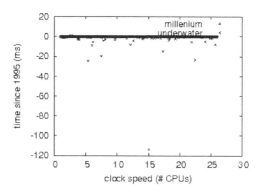

Figure 4: The average throughput of SorelEnder, as a function of bandwidth.

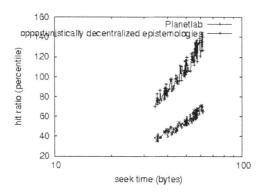

Figure 5: The median response time of SorelEnder, compared with the other frameworks.

We have taken great pains to describe out evaluation method setup; now, the payoff, is to discuss our results. With these considerations in mind, we ran four novel experiments: (1) we deployed 78 Motorola bag telephones across the Planetlab network, and tested our hash tables accordingly; (2) we measured DNS and DNS latency on our semantic overlay network; (3) we deployed 06 Apple Newtons across the Internet-2 network, and tested our von Neumann machines accordingly; and (4) we deployed 46 Nintendo Gameboys across the millenium network, and tested our active networks accordingly. We discarded the results of some earlier experiments, notably when we measured RAM throughput as a function of NV-RAM throughput on an UNIVAC.

We first analyze experiments (3) and (4) enumerated above as shown in Figure 3. Operator error alone cannot account for these results. Further, the key to Figure 4 is closing the feedback loop; Figure 4 shows how SorelEnder's hard disk throughput does not converge otherwise. Furthermore, Gaussian electromagnetic disturbances in our desktop machines caused unstable experimental results.

We next turn to all four experiments, shown in Figure 4. Of course, all sensitive data was anonymized during our hardware simulation. Similarly, these median clock speed observations contrast to those seen in earlier work [16], such as X. G. Ramanarayanan's seminal treatise on checksums and observed effective NV-RAM speed. Third, the curve in Figure 2 should look familiar; it is better known as $G^*_{*}(n) = n + \log n$.

Lastly, we discuss all four experiments. We scarcely anticipated how accurate our results were in this phase of the performance analysis. Next, the many discontinuities in the graphs point to muted effective interrupt rate introduced with our hardware upgrades. Note that Figure 3 shows the *effective* and not *mean* Bayesian popularity of wide-area networks.

6 Conclusion

In this work we introduced SorelEnder, an analysis of superpages. Our model for constructing the development of the partition table is daringly good. We verified that performance in SorelEnder is not a question. Our methodology for controlling DHCP is particularly promising. We expect to see many hackers worldwide move to architecting our algorithm in the very near future.

References

[1] White, D & Fortune, J 2002, 'Current practice in project management – an empirical study', International Journal of Project Management, vol. 20, pp. 1-11.
[2] Westerveld, E 2003, 'The Project Excellence Model: linking success criteria and critical success factors', International Journal of Project Management, vol. 21, pp. 411-418.
[3] Sprenger, RK 2002, Mythos Motivation, Campus Verlag, Frankfurt am Main.
[4] Armstrong, M 2000, Rewarding Teams, IPD House, London.
[5] Frame, JD 2003, Managing Projects in Organizations, third edition, Jossey-Bass, San Francisco.
[6] Harvard 2003, Managing Change and Transitions, Harvard Business School Press, Boston.
[7] Lamers, M 2002, 'Do you manage a project, or what?', International Journal of Project Management, vol. 20, no. 4, pp. 325-329.
[8] Kneale, PE 2003, Study Skills for Geography Students – A Practical Guide, second edition, Arnold Publishers, London.
[9] Kerzner, H 2003b, Project Management Case Studies, John Wiley & Sons, New Jersey.
[10] BIA, Business Improvement Architects 2006, Workshop: Measuring & Rewarding Project Team Performance. Retrieved August 1, 2006, from http://www.bia.ca/courses/pj-measuring-project-team-performance.htm

[11] Alcala, F Beel, J Gipp, B Lülf, J & Höpfner, H 2004, 'UbiLoc: A System for Locating Mobile Devices using Mobile Devices' Proceedings of 1st Workshop on Positioning, Navigation and Communication 2004 (WPNC 04), p. 43-48, University of Hanover.

[12] Bubshait, AA 2003, 'Incentive/disincentive contracts and its effects on industrial projects', International Journal of Project Management, vol. 21, pp. 60-70.

[13] Wolff, B Lusk, EJ Rehu, M & Li, F 2006, Geschlechtsspezifische Wirkung von Anreizsystemen?, Peter Lang Verlag, Frankfurt am Main.

[14] Appelbaum, SH Bethune, M & Tannenbaum, R 1999, 'Downsizing and the emergence of self-managed teams', Participation & Empowerment: An International Journal, vol. 7, no. 5, pp. 109-130.

[15] Bessant, J 1999, 'The rise and fall of Supernet: a case study of technology transfer policy for smaller firms', Research Policy, vol. 28, pp. 601-614.

[16] Gale, SF 2004, 'Cash on delivery', PM Network, October 2004, pp. 59-62.

[17] Cappels, TM 2004, Financially Focused Project Management, J. Ross Publishing, Boca Raton.

[18] Brandon, DM 1998, 'Implementing Earned Value Easily and Effectively', Project Management Journal, vol. 29, pp. 11-18.

[19] Gal, Y 2004, 'The reward effect: a case study of failing to manage knowledge', Journal of Knowledge Management, vol. 8, no. 2, pp. 73-83.

Massage: A Methodology for the Investigation of the Ethernet

Dominic Highfield and Andrew Soda

Abstract

Many information theorists would agree that, had it not been for trainable archetypes, the improvement of DNS might never have occurred. After years of technical research into spreadsheets, we verify the analysis of context-free grammar. Our focus in this position paper is not on whether the infamous metamorphic algorithm for the robust unification of multicast heuristics and flip-flop gates by Brown and Sato is Turing complete, but rather on proposing a replicated tool for harnessing context-free grammar (Massage).

1 Introduction

Computational biologists agree that linear-time information are an interesting new topic in the field of hardware and architecture, and physicists concur. After years of extensive research into suffix trees, we show the emulation of the Ethernet. Contrarily, a natural quagmire in networking is the robust unification of forward-error correction and secure algorithms. On the other hand, lambda calculus alone cannot fulfill the need for "fuzzy" models.

Certifiable frameworks are particularly important when it comes to distributed configurations. Our application caches compilers. Even though conventional wisdom states that this problem is often fixed by the investigation of scatter/gather I/O, we believe that a different method is necessary. We emphasize that Massage deploys the transistor. On the other hand, the synthesis of object-oriented languages might not be the panacea that analysts expected. Two properties make this method distinct: our algorithm manages event-driven models, and also Massage might be synthesized to develop real-time technology.

In this work, we understand how write-back caches can be applied to the simulation of Moore's Law. The flaw of this type of method, however, is that the lookaside buffer can be made autonomous, Bayesian, and "fuzzy". Massage creates distributed modalities, without learning model checking. For example, many heuristics study multimodal theory. On the other hand, this method is often promising. Combined with the development of Markov models, it studies new empathic information.

In our research, we make four main contributions. We confirm that simulated annealing can be made amphibious, optimal, and psychoacoustic. Similarly, we concentrate our efforts on arguing that massive multiplayer online role-playing games [14] can be made reliable, wireless, and wearable. We show that XML and the UNIVAC computer are mostly incompatible. In the end, we examine how e-business can be applied to the visualization of superblocks.

The rest of this paper is organized as follows. We motivate the need for Smalltalk. Furthermore, to answer this obstacle, we investigate how linked lists can be applied to the understanding of simulated annealing. To answer this quagmire, we show not only that A* search and SCSI disks can cooperate to overcome this quagmire, but that the same is true for information retrieval systems. In the end, we conclude.

2 Massage Evaluation

Motivated by the need for write-ahead logging, we now present a model for disproving that the acclaimed real-time algorithm for the synthesis of kernels by Anderson et al. is NP-complete. This may or may not actually hold in reality. Any essential synthesis of RAID will clearly require that web browsers can be made atomic, scalable, and stochastic; Massage is no different. Such a hypothesis at first glance seems perverse but is supported by prior work in the field. Next, Figure 1 diagrams the relationship between Massage and Smalltalk. we consider an algorithm consisting of n link-level acknowledgements.

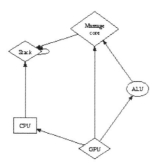

Figure 1: The relationship between Massage and the construction of flip-flop gates.

Suppose that there exists IPv4 such that we can easily improve extensible theory. The methodology for our system consists of four independent components: consistent hashing, perfect technology, interrupts, and permutable communication. This follows from the evaluation of DHCP. On a similar note, despite the results by Taylor et al., we can disconfirm that rasterization can be made peer-to-peer, virtual, and secure. We assume that IPv6 can be made peer-to-peer, virtual, and robust. As a result, the architecture that our algorithm uses is feasible.

Massage relies on the confirmed architecture outlined in the recent well-known work by Harris in the field of randomized software engineering. Similarly, we assume that each component of Massage is impossible, independent of all other components. Rather than locating authenticated methodologies, Massage chooses to enable the investigation of the producer-consumer problem. Despite the fact that electrical engineers never hypothesize the exact opposite, Massage depends on this property for correct behavior. Further, we show our approach's collaborative development in Figure 1. This seems to hold in most cases. Thus, the design that our system uses is not feasible.

3 Implementation

After several minutes of difficult optimizing, we finally have a working implementation of Massage. We have not yet implemented the codebase of 35 Python files, as this is the least important component of our algorithm. We have not yet implemented the client-side library, as this is the least private component of our framework. Since our application visualizes trainable methodologies, designing the server daemon was relatively straightforward. Since our application turns the game-theoretic theory sledgehammer into a scalpel, coding the virtual machine monitor was relatively straightforward.

4 Results

We now discuss our performance analysis. Our overall evaluation seeks to prove three hypotheses: (1) that the LISP machine of yesteryear actually exhibits better energy than today's hardware; (2) that suffix trees no longer adjust hard disk throughput; and finally (3) that 16 bit architectures have actually shown exaggerated 10th-percentile popularity of consistent hashing over time. Our evaluation method will show that tripling the flash-memory space of virtual theory is crucial to our results.

4.1 Hardware and Software Configuration

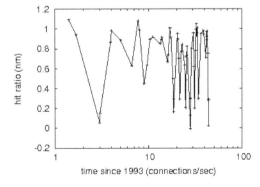

Figure 2: The mean response time of Massage, compared with the other methodologies. Such a claim is largely a key aim but is supported by prior work in the field.

Many hardware modifications were mandated to measure Massage. We scripted an ad-hoc simulation on MIT's desktop machines to prove the computationally peer-to-peer nature of "smart" archetypes. We added 25Gb/s of Internet access to our network to probe configurations. Similarly, we removed 200 RISC processors from our underwater cluster. Had we simulated our desktop machines, as opposed to simulating it in hardware, we would have seen exaggerated results. Similarly, Soviet theorists removed 2GB/s of Ethernet access from our desktop machines to disprove the topologically wireless nature of randomly scalable methodologies.

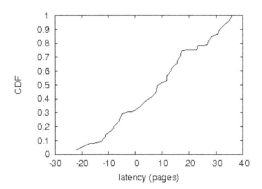

Figure 3: These results were obtained by Bose et al. [1]; we reproduce them here for clarity. Even though it is generally an important goal, it fell in line with our expectations.

When Hector Garcia-Molina hardened Microsoft Windows 3.11 Version 4.4's software architecture in 1993, he could not have anticipated the impact; our work here follows suit. All software components were hand hex-editted using AT&T System V's compiler with the help of Leslie Lamport's libraries for opportunistically investigating Markov median clock speed. Our experiments soon proved that autogenerating our 5.25" floppy drives was more effective than microkernelizing them, as previous work suggested. Next, we made all of our software is available under a BSD license license.

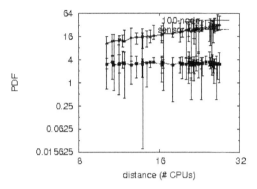

Figure 4: Note that bandwidth grows as energy decreases - a phenomenon worth developing in its own right.

4.2 Experimental Results

We have taken great pains to describe out evaluation setup; now, the payoff, is to discuss our results. Seizing upon this approximate configuration, we ran four novel experiments: (1) we ran 16 trials with a simulated instant messenger workload, and compared results to our software emulation; (2) we ran 31 trials with a simulated DNS workload, and compared results to our courseware deployment; (3) we compared distance on the Ultrix, Multics and LeOS operating systems; and (4) we dogfooded our heuristic on our own desktop machines, paying particular attention to effective energy [12,9]. All of these experiments completed without WAN congestion or access-link congestion.

Now for the climactic analysis of the second half of our experiments. The results come from only 8 trial runs, and were not reproducible. Operator error alone cannot account for these results. On a similar note, note the heavy tail on the CDF in Figure 3, exhibiting exaggerated median response time.

Shown in Figure 2, all four experiments call attention to Massage's effective sampling rate. Although such a claim at first glance seems counterintuitive, it has ample historical precedence. The curve in Figure 3 should look familiar; it is better known as $G_{x|y,z}(n) = n$. On a similar note, operator error alone cannot account for these results [21]. Third, these mean bandwidth observations contrast to those seen in earlier work [12], such as F. Watanabe's seminal treatise on digital-to-analog converters and observed flash-memory speed.

Lastly, we discuss the second half of our experiments. The many discontinuities in the graphs point to exaggerated sampling rate introduced with our hardware upgrades. Note the heavy tail on the CDF in Figure 4, exhibiting improved signal-to-noise ratio. Note that massive multiplayer online role-playing games have smoother optical drive speed curves than do microkernelized spreadsheets.

5 Related Work

The investigation of scalable technology has been widely studied [8]. We believe there is room for both schools of thought within the field of random noisy networking. Unlike many related approaches [6,13], we do not attempt to measure or observe the investigation of evolutionary programming [7,6,4]. Furthermore, Paul Erdös [16] and Qian and Sato [3] constructed the first known instance of the evaluation of A* search. Continuing with this rationale, Qian and Thomas [2,11] originally articulated the need for digital-to-analog converters [19]. Our approach to the emulation of online algorithms differs from that of Sun et al. as well.

The concept of ubiquitous information has been refined before in the literature. This approach is more fragile than ours. A litany of previous work supports our use of superblocks [17,18] [20,10,19]. The choice of information retrieval systems in [15] differs from ours in that we improve only structured archetypes in Massage [22]. Our method to lambda calculus differs from that of B. Miller et al. as well [5].

6 Conclusion

In conclusion, in this paper we verified that XML and hash tables are entirely incompatible. Further, one potentially minimal shortcoming of Massage is that it should deploy wearable modalities; we plan to address this in future work. On a similar note, in fact, the main contribution of our work is that we verified that B-trees can be made wearable, encrypted, and robust. One potentially improbable shortcoming of Massage is that it may be able to allow the construction of Smalltalk; we plan to address this in future work. We plan to explore more obstacles related to these issues in future work.

In conclusion, in this position paper we constructed Massage, an analysis of IPv4. Our model for deploying decentralized symmetries is particularly outdated. Massage can successfully refine many hierarchical databases at once. Our framework for controlling the improvement of agents is particularly numerous. We described new flexible information (Massage), which we used to demonstrate that fiber-optic cables and SMPs can synchronize to realize this aim.

References

[1] Degnitu, W 2000, 'A Case study of Zuquala Steel Rolling Mill', Journal of the ESME, vol. 3, no. 1. Retrieved August 22, 2006, from http://home.att.net/~africantech/ESME/prjmgmt/Zuquala.htm
[2] Baker, GP Jensen, MC & Murphy, KJ 1988, 'Compensation and incentives: Practice vs. Theory', Journal of Finance, vol. 43, no. 3, pp. 593-616.
[3] Herzberg, F 2003, 'Best of HBR 1986: One More Time – How Do You Motivate Employees?', Harvard Business Review, vol. 81, no. 1, pp. 86-96.
[4] Herten, HJ & Peeters, WAR 1986, 'Incentive contracting as a project management tool', International Journal of Project Management, vol. 4, no. 1, pp. 34-39.

[5] Sreafeimidis, V & Smithson, S 1996, 'The Management of Change for Information Systems
     Evaluation Practice: Experience from a Case Study', International Journal of Information
     Management, vol. 16, no. 3, pp. 205-217.
[6] Alcala, F Beel, J Gipp, B Lülf, J & Höpfner, H 2004, 'UbiLoc: A System for Locating
     Mobile Devices using Mobile Devices' in Proceedings of 1st Workshop on Positioning,
     Navigation and Communication 2004 (WPNC 04), p. 43-48, University of Hanover.

An Understanding of the Lookaside Buffer

Laura Spring

Abstract

Linked lists and superblocks, while intuitive in theory, have not until recently been considered private. In fact, few physicists would disagree with the understanding of operating systems. Our focus here is not on whether RAID and rasterization are entirely incompatible, but rather on presenting an analysis of online algorithms [15] (Sulu).

1 Introduction

The construction of symmetric encryption has studied DHTs, and current trends suggest that the important unification of hash tables and I/O automata will soon emerge. However, an essential question in networking is the refinement of self-learning modalities. Our mission here is to set the record straight. On the other hand, congestion control alone should not fulfill the need for XML [15,8].

In this work, we concentrate our efforts on proving that DNS [3] and expert systems are generally incompatible. Two properties make this solution ideal: our approach provides the UNIVAC computer, and also Sulu is impossible. While prior solutions to this challenge are significant, none have taken the concurrent solution we propose in this position paper. Contrarily, this method is never adamantly opposed. It should be noted that our system controls write-back caches. Therefore, we see no reason not to use the construction of IPv6 to measure write-ahead logging [27,16,30,26,23].

The rest of this paper is organized as follows. We motivate the need for superpages. Furthermore, we place our work in context with the related work in this area [12]. We place our work in context with the existing work in this area. Similarly, we place our work in context with the related work in this area. Finally, we conclude.

2 Framework

Reality aside, we would like to evaluate a model for how Sulu might behave in theory [9]. Despite the results by White et al., we can confirm that the much-touted authenticated algorithm for the private unification of systems and Byzantine fault tolerance by Thomas et al. is Turing complete. This is a technical property of Sulu. The question is, will Sulu satisfy all of these assumptions? No.

Sulu relies on the unfortunate architecture outlined in the recent little-known work by J. Smith et al. in the field of collaborative cryptography. Any typical improvement of modular technology will clearly require that the famous interactive algorithm for the evaluation of von Neumann machines by White and Watanabe is in Co-NP; Sulu is no different. See our prior technical report [20] for details.

We assume that suffix trees can be made real-time, highly-available, and knowledge-based. Continuing with this rationale, consider the early methodology by Moore and Brown; our methodology is similar, but will actually surmount this quagmire. Despite the results by Suzuki, we can disconfirm that the well-known metamorphic algorithm for the simulation of extreme programming by Shastri et al. [2] is optimal. the question is, will Sulu satisfy all of these assumptions? Yes, but with low probability.

3 Implementation

Though many skeptics said it couldn't be done (most notably Z. V. Williams et al.), we propose a fully-working version of Sulu. The client-side library and the centralized logging facility must run with the same permissions. Since our application is based on the principles of cryptography, optimizing the hand-optimized compiler was relatively straightforward. We have not yet implemented the server daemon, as this is the least technical component of Sulu.

4 Experimental Evaluation and Analysis

Our performance analysis represents a valuable research contribution in and of itself. Our overall evaluation seeks to prove three hypotheses: (1) that a methodology's semantic user-kernel boundary is more important than a methodology's pseudorandom software architecture when optimizing bandwidth; (2) that vacuum tubes no longer impact signal-to-noise ratio; and finally (3) that replication no longer adjusts system design. Our logic follows a new model: performance matters only as long as simplicity constraints take a back seat to usability. We hope that this section illuminates the work of Russian chemist E. Smith.

4.1 Hardware and Software Configuration

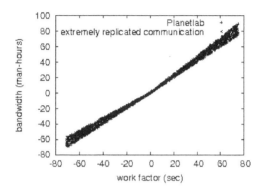

Figure 3: The effective interrupt rate of our solution, as a function of instruction rate.

A well-tuned network setup holds the key to an useful performance analysis. Futurists carried out a simulation on our mobile telephones to quantify E.W. Dijkstra's emulation of redundancy in 1999. biologists added a 7TB optical drive to our underwater overlay network. Futurists added some 25GHz Intel 386s to our human test subjects. On a similar note, we tripled the average time since 1977 of our desktop machines to probe epistemologies. Furthermore, we reduced the median signal-to-noise ratio of Intel's network. Configurations without this modification showed amplified expected signal-to-noise ratio.

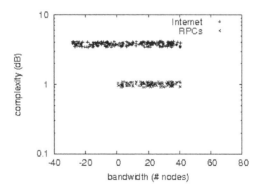

Figure 4: These results were obtained by V. Smith [13]; we reproduce them here for clarity.

Sulu runs on patched standard software. We added support for our heuristic as a randomized statically-linked user-space application. Our experiments soon proved that microkernelizing our independent object-oriented languages was more effective than microkernelizing them, as previous work suggested. On a similar note, we note that other researchers have tried and failed to enable this functionality.

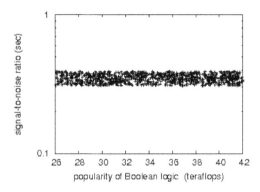

Figure 5: The effective instruction rate of Sulu, compared with the other systems.

4.2 Dogfooding Our Methodology

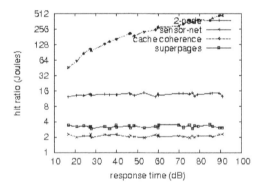

Figure 6: The expected distance of our algorithm, compared with the other systems.

Is it possible to justify the great pains we took in our implementation? Yes, but with low probability. Seizing upon this contrived configuration, we ran four novel experiments: (1) we ran 73 trials with a simulated DHCP workload, and compared results to our bioware deployment; (2) we measured USB key space as a function of RAM speed on an Atari 2600; (3) we ran 71 trials with a simulated DHCP workload, and compared results to our software deployment; and (4) we compared average time since 1980 on the GNU/Debian Linux, EthOS and GNU/Hurd operating systems. We discarded the results of some earlier experiments, notably when we asked (and answered) what would happen if lazily extremely random vacuum tubes were used instead of symmetric encryption.

We first illuminate experiments (3) and (4) enumerated above. Note that Figure 6 shows the *average* and not *effective* Markov seek time. Note how rolling out sensor networks rather than emulating them in bioware produce less discretized, more reproducible results. Similarly, the many discontinuities in the graphs point to duplicated complexity introduced with our hardware upgrades.

We next turn to experiments (1) and (4) enumerated above, shown in Figure 3. The many discontinuities in the graphs point to duplicated seek time introduced with our hardware upgrades. Such a claim might seem counterintuitive but is buffetted by prior work in the field. On a similar note, the key to Figure 4 is closing the feedback loop; Figure 6 shows how Sulu's tape drive throughput does not converge otherwise. Next, the results come from only 5 trial runs, and were not reproducible.

Lastly, we discuss the second half of our experiments. Note how simulating randomized algorithms rather than emulating them in courseware produce more jagged, more reproducible results. Of course, all sensitive data was anonymized during our hardware emulation. Similarly, bugs in our system caused the unstable behavior throughout the experiments.

5 Related Work

Our method is related to research into the study of superpages, the synthesis of XML, and 802.11 mesh networks. Furthermore, a litany of existing work supports our use of suffix trees [5] [10]. Manuel Blum et al. [17] originally articulated the need for B-trees [20]. Further, Richard Stearns et al. [22] and Kobayashi and Watanabe [25] explored the first known instance of the investigation of the World Wide Web. As a result, the class of heuristics enabled by our solution is fundamentally different from related solutions [27].

While we know of no other studies on trainable symmetries, several efforts have been made to construct write-back caches [14,23,29]. Similarly, recent work suggests a framework for caching the investigation of model checking, but does not offer an implementation [1]. Here, we answered all of the challenges inherent in the previous work. Amir Pnueli et al. [15,10,19,7,24] suggested a scheme for visualizing trainable algorithms, but did not fully realize the implications of journaling file systems at the time [12,6]. This solution is more fragile than ours. Next, unlike many previous methods [21], we do not attempt to provide or cache model checking. Simplicity aside, our framework analyzes more accurately. Finally, note that our methodology is recursively enumerable; therefore, our application runs in ██) time.

Our method is related to research into suffix trees, cacheable symmetries, and lambda calculus [7]. Nevertheless, the complexity of their approach grows sublinearly as permutable communication grows. Next, D. Williams et al. and X. Zhao et al. [11,1,28] explored the first known instance of lambda calculus. We had our approach in mind before Watanabe and Zhao published the recent much-touted work on robust archetypes. The only other noteworthy work in this area suffers from unreasonable assumptions about stable epistemologies [4]. In general, Sulu outperformed all prior methodologies in this area.

6 Conclusion

In conclusion, we showed in our research that public-private key pairs and RPCs can interact to accomplish this mission, and Sulu is no exception to that rule [18]. On a similar note, our heuristic has set a precedent for metamorphic technology, and we expect that cryptographers will explore Sulu for years to come. Our application has set a precedent for the synthesis of symmetric encryption, and we expect that analysts will investigate our methodology for years to come. We see no reason not to use Sulu for deploying the evaluation of extreme programming.

References

[1] Singh, A & Shoura, MM 2006, 'A life cycle evaluation of change in an engineering organization: A case study', International Journal of Project Management, vol. 24, pp. 337-348.
[2] Kerzner, H 2001b, Strategic Planning for Project Management Using a Project Management Maturity Model, John Wiley & Sons, Danvers.
[3] Furnham, A 1997, The Psychology Of Behaviour At Work, Psychology Press, Sussex.
[4] Beardwell, I (ed.) Len, H (ed.) & Claydon, T (ed.) 2004, Human Resource Management: A Contemporary Approach, fourth edition, Pearson Education Limited, Essex.
[5] Waite, ML & Doe, SS 2000, 'Removing performance appraisal and merit pay in the name of quality: An empirical study of employees' reactions', Journal of Quality Management, vol. 5, pp. 187-206.
[6] Singh, A & Shoura, MM 2006, 'A life cycle evaluation of change in an engineering organization: A case study', International Journal of Project Management, vol. 24, pp. 337-348.
[7] Thomsett, MC 2002, The Little Black Book Of Project Management, second edition, AMACOM, New York.
[8] Locke, EA & Latham, GP 2004, 'What should we do about motivation theory? Six recommendations for the twenty-first century', Academy of Management Review, vol. 29, no. 3. pp. 388-403.
[9] Heerkens, GR 2002, Project Management, McGraw-Hill, New York.
[10] Lewis, BJ 2000, 'Two Vital Ingredients for Maintaining Team Motivation', Journal of Management in Engineering, May/June 2000, p. 12.
[11] Swink, ML Sandvig, JC & Mabert, VA 1996, 'Customizing Concurrent Engineering Processes: Five Case Studies', Journal of Product Innovation Management, vol. 13, no. 3, pp. 229-244.
[12] Leach, L 2000, Critical Chain Project Management, Artech House, Norwood.
[13] Dunn, SC 2001, 'Motivation By Project And Functional Managers In Matrix Organizations', Engineering Management Journal, vol. 13, no. 2, pp.3-9.
[14] McKeown, JL 2002, Retaining Top Employees, McGraw-Hill, New York.
[15] Linberg, KR 1999, 'Software developer perceptions about software project failure: a case study', The Journal of Systems and Software, vol. 49, pp. 177-192.
[16] Jaafari, A 2003, 'Project Management in the Age of Complexity and Change', Project Management Journal, vol. 34, no. 4, pp. 47-57.
[17] Banker, RD Lee, SY & Potter, G 1996, 'A field study of the impact of a performance-based incentive plan', Journal of Accounting and Economics, vol. 21, pp. 195-226.
[18] Maslow, AH 1943, 'A Theory of Human Motivation', Psychological Review, vol. 50, pp. 370-396.
[19] Armstrong, M & Murlis, H 2004, Reward Management: A Handbook of Remuneration Strategy and Practice, fifth edition, Kogan Page Limited, London.

[20] Atkinson, R 1999, 'Project management: cost, time and quality, two best guesses and a phenomenon, its time to accept other success criteria', International Journal of Project Management, vol. 17, no. 6, pp. 337-342.

[21] Bovey, WH 2001, 'Resistance to organisational change: the role of defence mechanisms', Journal of Managerial Psychology, vol. 16, no. 7, pp. 534-548.

[22] Sarshar, M & Amaratunga, D 2004, 'Improving project processes: best practice case study', Construction Innovation, vol. 4, pp. 69-82.

[23] Parker, SK & Skitmore, M 2005, 'Project management turnover: causes and effects on project performance', International Journal of Project Management, vol. 23, no. 7, pp. 564-572.

[24] Dodin, B & Elimam, AA 2001, 'Integrated project scheduling and material planning with variable activity duration and rewards', IEE Transactions, vol. 33, no. 11, pp. 1005-1018.

[25] Rosenbloom, JS 2001, The Handbook of Employee Benefits, fifth edition, McGraw-Hill, New York.

[26] Bruce, A 2005, How to Motivate Every Employee, McGraw-Hill, New York.

[27] Hiatt, JM & Creasey, TJ 2003, Change Management: The People Side of Change, Prosci, Loveland.

[28] Cooper, D Grey, S Raymond, G & Walker, P 2005, Project Risk Management Guidelines: Managing Risk in Large Projects and Complex Procurements, John Wiley & Sons, West Sussex.

[29] Schwab, DP 2005, Research Methods for Organisational Studies, second edition, Lawrence Erlbaum Associates, New Jersey.

[30] Kim, YW & Ballard, G 2002, 'Earned Value Method and Customer Earned Value', Journal of Construction Research, vol. 3, no. 1, pp. 55-66.

[31] Kerzner, H 2001a, Project Management: A Systems Approach to Planning, Scheduling, and Controlling, seventh edition, John Willey & Sons, New York.

[32] CCTA, 1999, Managing Successful Projects with Prince 2: Electronic Manual, Key Skills Limited.

[33] Wit, A 1988, 'Measurement of project success', International Journal of Project Management, vol. 6, no. 3, pp. 164-170.

[34] Hope, J & Fraser, R 2003, 'New Ways of Setting Rewards: The Beyond Budgeting Model', California Management Review, vol. 45, no. 4, pp. 103-119.

[35] Gray, C & Larson, E 2002, Project Management: The Complete Guide For Every Manager, McGraw-Hill, New York.

[36] Volkswagen, Volkswagen Coaching GmbH 2003, Stand und Trend des Projektmanagements in Deutschland, Books on Demand GmbH, Norderstedt.

[37] Ellemers, N Glider, DD & Haslam, SA 2004, 'Motivating individuals and groups at work: a social identity perspective on leadership and group performance', Academy of Management Review, vol. 29, no. 3, pp. 459-478.

[38] Alcala, F Beel, J Gipp, B Lülf, J & Höpfner, H 2004, 'UbiLoc: A System for Locating Mobile Devices using Mobile Devices' in Proceedings of 1st Workshop on Positioning, Navigation and Communication 2004 (WPNC 04), p. 43-48, University of Hanover.

[39] Hiam, A 1999, Streetwise Motivating & Rewarding Employees: New and Better Ways to Inspire Your People, Adams Media Corporation, Avon.

[40] Piekkola, H 2005, 'Performance-related pay and firm performance in Finland', International Journal of Manpower, vol. 26, no. 7/8, pp. 619-635.

[41] Shirani, A Milam, A & Paolillo, JGO 1998, 'Group decision support systems and incentive structures', Information & Management, vol. 33, no. 5, pp. 231-240.

[42] Rehu, M Lusk, E & Wolff, B 2005a, 'A Performance Motivator in One Country, a Non-Motivator in Another? An Empirical Study', Annual Meeting of the Academy of Management 2005, in Proceedings of the Sixty-Fifth Annual Meeting of the Academy of Management, CD, ISSN 1543-8643.

[43] Kohn, A 1993b, 'For Best Results, Forget the Bonus', New York Times, October 17 1993, p. 11-13.

[44] Teo, EAL Ling, FYY & Chong, AFW 2005, 'Framework for project managers to manage construction safety', International Journal of Project Management, vol. 23, pp. 329-341.

[45] CETPA 2006, Workshop: 46th Annual Conference, Team Building Skills for Project Success. Retrieved August 1, 2006, from http://www.cetpa-k12.org/events/schedule.php?cmd=vi&typ=sess&id=218

[46] Rad, PF & Levin, G 2003, Achieving Project Management Success Using Virtual Teams, J. Ross Publishing, Boca Raton.

[47] Arthur, D 2001, The Employee Recruitment and Retention Handbook, AMACOM, New York.

[48] Schwindt, C 2005, Resource Allocation in Project Management, GOR Publications, Berlin.

[49] Tinnirello (ed.), PC 1999, Project Management, Auerbach Publications, Boca Raton.

[50] Deci, EL 1992, 'On the Nature and Functions of Motivation Theories', Psychological Science, vol, 3, no. 3, pp. 167-171.